C000163064

SWIMMING
FOR PEOPLE WITH
DISABILITIES

Second Edition

Association of
Swimming Therapy

Preface by Rolf Harris A.M. O.B.E.
Foreword by Elizabeth Dendy M.B.E.

A & C BLACK · LONDON

Published by A & C Black
(Publishers) Ltd
35 Bedford Row, London WC1R 4JH

2nd edition 1992
Reprinted 1994
First published 1981, under the title of
Swimming for the Disabled
Reprinted 1984

© Association of Swimming Therapy
1981, 1992

ISBN 0 7136 3441 3

A CIP catalogue record for this book
is available from the British Library.

Typeset by ABM Typographics Ltd, Hull
Printed and bound in Great Britain by
Biddles Ltd, Guildford and King's Lynn

Contents

Preface

I have been swimming all my life it seems, having learnt when I was about three and a half or quarter to four. Our house was on the banks of the river Swan in Western Australia and during the 20 odd years that I lived there, nothing pleased me more than to teach other youngsters to swim. I particularly loved the magical moment when a non-swimmer finally decided to trust and believe you, do what you said and suddenly realised that what you said *was* true . . . they actually *could* float! The thrill you shared with them made it all worth while.

I have continued to pester non-swimmers all my adult life, urging them to listen to logic, to take the big breath, put their face down in the water, relax and lie there long enough to feel the buoyancy of their body being supported in and by the water. I love it.

At present I am President of PHAB – the Physically Handicapped and Able Bodied – in the UK. When I see the work carried out by the Association of Swimming Therapy I wish I had taken my love of swimming further and found out about helping people with a disability to learn to swim.

I stand in amazement when I see the simplicity and obvious logic in what the AST does and the way it does it. I take my hat off to all the dedicated people who have made these creative and inventive teaching methods a reality.

Rolf Harris A.M. O.B.E.

Foreword

It is interesting to look back over more than a decade to 1981 – the International Year of Disabled People – when the first edition of this book was published. What have we achieved in this time? Have opportunities for people with disabilities to take part in swimming increased?

At the top level of performance the answer must be 'Yes'. Standards have risen significantly, due largely to the involvement of coaches and swimming clubs, the improved level of training provided and the identification and early development of talent, mainly carried out in the clubs, such as those run by the Association of Swimming Therapy (AST). The high profile of the Paralympics has increased awareness of the outstanding ability of swimmers with disabilities. More swimmers are taking part in competition at all levels; probably the greatest increase is among people with learning difficulties, who were for so long deprived of opportunities in sport.

We do not know how many people with disabilities swim. If this is because many of them swim with family and friends outside the special clubs and sessions, we should welcome the integration. Numbers of swimmers in the special clubs continue to increase, highlighting the contribution made by thousands of volunteers. The new edition of this book demonstrates the expertise, experience and multi-professional skills which exist within the AST.

Much remains to be done before people with disabilities have equal opportunities with other swimmers. There are still too many organisations working in isolation. The result is often duplication of effort, overlap and confusion. The National Co-ordinating Committee includes all the major organisations, and it is pleasing to see the positive contribution now being made by the swimming organisations – the Amateur Swimming Association (ASA), the English Schools Swimming Association (ESSA) and the Royal Life Saving Society (RLSS) – as well as the facility providers.

The report of the Minister for Sport's review on sport for people with disabilities – 'Building on Ability' – recommends that responsibility should ultimately rest with mainstream sport. Few would disagree with this recommendation and it is encouraging that organisations such as the AST are ready and willing to share their unique experience and expertise with the governing bodies. The development of the National Vocational Qualification (NVQ) for swimming will be under the aegis of the ASA; consultation is taking place so that all relevant expertise is taken into account in arriving at the final system.

With this type of co-operation we can look to the future with confidence. *Swimming for People with Disabilities* will add significantly to the knowledge required for continued progress. I wish it well.

Elizabeth Dendy

Elizabeth Dendy M.B.E.
National liaison with sport for people with disabilities –
The Sports Council

Acknowledgements

This book is based on the Halliwick Method which was devised by James McMillan M.B.E, who continues to develop the method with his research work, helping us to understand more about what is happening to the human body in water. We thank him for all we have learnt from him, for the enormous contribution he has made to this field of work, benefiting people with disabilities and those who work with them in the water, and for his continued support.

Our thanks are also due to many others who are too numerous to mention by name. However, we do wish to record our thanks to Jim Kibart for some of the original diagrams from the first edition, and to Bill Latto, Andrew Davie and Anthony Fisher for their painstaking photographic work. Above all, we are deeply indebted to Haro for generously giving his excellent drawings.

Introduction

This book is about having fun in the water. While it is mainly concerned with people with disabilities, it will help people of all ages who are learning to swim to find the joy of independence in the water in safety.

Swimming for People with Disabilities will, we hope, encourage those whose lives are restricted by their disability to take to the water. It will broaden the horizons of their existence. For many, courage and determination can lead to greater independence.

The word 'fun' has been stressed and may mean games, races, galas, competitions, open water swimming, diving, etc. The sheer exhilaration of discarding the physical burdens necessary for life on land and entering the water, will in itself be a satisfying achievement. This sense of freedom and accomplishment can be a great morale booster in everyday life.

For people with disabilities, swimming is both remedial and recreational, but it can also be social. The obvious satisfaction of meeting others with a like interest is a tremendous asset to those who may often be lonely in their own homes.

Happily, today there are many organisations concerned with swimming for people with disabilities. In a club situation, voluntary help can be provided by lifeguards, first-aiders such as the St. John Ambulance Brigade and the Red Cross, the Rotarians, Lions, Guides, Scouts, and individuals working for their Duke of Edinburgh Award. For all would-be instructors, practice and water experience is vital.

This book has been written in the hope that helpers and instructors in clubs, and professional people who organise swimming sessions in schools, hospitals and training centres will understand the enormous benefits that can result in the use of the special method taught throughout the book – the Halliwick Method.

Note   Throughout the book swimmers and instructors are referred to individually as 'he'. This should, of course, be taken to mean 'he or she' where appropriate.

1

The Halliwick Method and the AST

The AST has, since its inception in the early 1950s, worked at promoting all aspects of swimming for people with a disability. Its aims are to teach water happiness, pool safety and swimming, to help form new swimming clubs, and to encourage people with a disability to use the water.

Swimming for People with Disabilities is about the work of the AST and the Halliwick Method and how the AST and its volunteers use the method to teach people to enjoy the water irrespective of their type or degree of disability.

The Halliwick Method is unique to the AST. It was developed by James McMillan M.B.E, who is now President Emeritus of the association. Work first started in 1949 in London at the Halliwick school, after which the method has been named. The method is now practised in clubs all over the world. The association has more than 130 affiliated clubs and many personal affiliates. Wherever there is a need and a facility, the AST will help to form new clubs and to support its affiliates. There are also international links on every continent. James McMillan himself works from Switzerland.

The work that the Halliwick Method started in 1949 continues to develop. It is based on the scientific principles of hydrostatics, hydrodynamics and body mechanics, but is not a static set of principles: it lives and grows as its members develop their own skills and share their discoveries. While members do not need to have a full understanding of the scientific ground rules to work or even learn successfully in the water, the concepts underlie every action. The activities which the method teaches encompass such skills as learning to feel at home in the water, breath control (including the ability to stand up and recover to a safe breathing position), an understanding of how upthrust and turbulence affect the body and how to respond, as well as balance, sculling and the development of basic strokes.

The recreational aspects of swimming particularly are much emphasised so that the water sessions are not only practical and

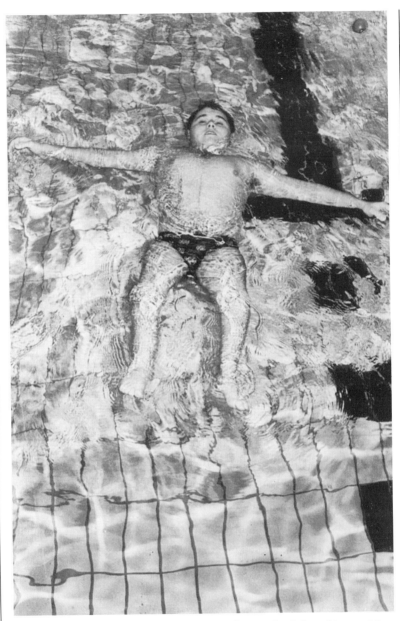

1   The water-happy swimmer in the back float and safe breathing position

constructive but also fun. Up-to-date teaching methods and games, either in groups or single pairs, help to make them so.

Everyone being taught is called a 'swimmer'. Until the swimmer has achieved proficiency and confidence, he will always be accompanied, on a one-to-one basis, by an instructor. Swimmers are usually taught as part of a small group. Group work is structured and led by a group leader. Learning is enhanced by working in a group and is made more fun.

Fig. 1 Buoyancy aids can unbalance a swimmer, upset his confidence in the water's support, and if they leak . . .

No flotation or artificial buoyancy aids are used. The swimmer has to learn how to make the most of his own development and to find and control his own natural balance.

While the Halliwick Method itself is used by professionals as well as volunteers, the AST instructors all work on a voluntary basis. Like other voluntary organisations, the AST uses many methods to increase the level of volunteer help. It has found that the relationships fostered in a club situation often continue outside club hours.

2

Adjustment to water

We all meet changes in our lives and have to come to terms with them. We go to school, start work, get married, travel abroad or venture into other unfamiliar territories which can be strange and worrying; we all react and adapt in different ways and at different rates.

Building confidence

Swimming should be fun and first impressions are important. The atmosphere of your club or group could greatly influence someone about to join. The reception he receives from the bathside helper or instructor, with regard to friendliness, patience and correct support, provides the foundation on which confidence can be built. Without confidence, progress will be slow and a swimmer may give up coming to your club.

Talking relieves tensions, diverts attention from worries and can induce relaxation and better buoyancy. It may be difficult to communicate with some swimmers but every effort should be made not only by the spoken word but also through facial expressions, singing or physical contact. Eye contact, smiling and effective communication establish the rapport between instructor and swimmer that is such an important springboard to water confidence.

In general, instructors should be aware that the volume of noise and boisterous activity in the pool could be daunting to a newcomer – some may need two or three visits and much persuasion before venturing into the water. A nervous swimmer will need help to recognise his potential ability in the water. The instructor's role is clear: to teach safety skills and to make sure that the swimmer feels he can trust the support that the water gives and rely on the instructor's assistance.

The opposite problem to a lack of self-confidence is a lack of understanding of danger or the depth of water. This is especially great if the swimmer is physically capable and mobile. While some level of mental adjustment can be achieved via experience and repetition, the instructor of such a swimmer must be very alert at all times and capable of moving as quickly as the swimmer!

Instructor guidelines

Instructors should always remember that not only are they continually assessing their swimmers, but that the swimmers in their turn are taking stock of their instructors. Instructors who fail to communicate, offer incorrect support or prevent a swimmer's progress towards independence, will not gain the swimmer's trust and confidence. This would close the door to a realm of social, mobile and competitive activity that his disabilities may have prevented him from pursuing on land.

How can the instructor keep the door open? The right attitudes to both the water and the swimmer are the first consideration and are based on caring common sense; for instance, appreciating that a partially paralysed swimmer may feel the cold more than someone who can warm up easily. Instructors must feel satisfied that they are completely in control in the depth and area of water in which they are working, regardless of what is happening around them. They must assume total responsibility for the welfare of their swimmer.

The instructor should stay with his swimmer at all times (except in some group activities), until that swimmer is assessed as safe and independent.

The instructor and swimmer do all underwater activities together and so the instructor needs to be proficient enough in these skills to be able to teach by example. An instructor should always be prepared to open his eyes under the water before asking a swimmer to do likewise. Anyone not prepared to do this would not make a suitable instructor.

The instructor should understand the mechanics of being in water. He must be aware of his own body position, of the importance of breathing control, of the effects of pressure and density and how movement patterns are created and controlled.

Correct entries, exits and behaviour in the water are best taught by example. Therefore, the instructor's entries and exits should be the same as those taught to the swimmers. Extrovert behaviour highlights ability differences and can lead to accidents through swimmers trying to copy bad practices.

The process of disengagement

Gradually a swimmer should be encouraged to reduce his reliance on the instructor and to become more independent in the water.

While no skill can be taught from the begining to maximum ability without assistance, no skill can be fully aquired and used if assistance is always present. The aim is for physical and mental disengagement. To be effective and to allow full mental adjustment, disengagement depends on a positive attitude from the instructor.

Learning how to observe and assess the minimum level of assistance required by the swimmer at every stage of teaching is a very important skill. To start with, think about the swimmer's entry. If full assistance is always offered there is no progress towards independence (see chapter 4).

Each new skill needs full assistance to start with, then a progression through partial, minimal and, finally, no physical support. Even when no support is needed, the instructor must be constantly on the alert without the swimmer being necessarily aware of it. There should not be a sudden lunge after the instructor realises the swimmer has lost control!

Remember that a swimmer falls more slowly in water than in air because of water's higher density. There is time to think and time to act to correct the fall, with the instructor offering any needed advice. The instructor's hands need not be in physical contact with the swimmer's body but should be in the correct position – a fraction away from the swimmer – to offer support when it is needed.

A nervous swimmer may rely on eye contact for reassurance and security in his initial stages of learning. It is a big step in disengagement, then, when both swimmer and instructor can face in the same direction while maintaining physical contact.

Swimmers should be discouraged from becoming too dependent on a particular instructor; practising activities which involve the interchange of swimmers and instructors can make this easier.

In group activities, further stages of disengagement can be explored where swimmers can support each other under close supervision. This encourages independence as well as responsibility to others.

For a swimmer with a severe disability, dependent on a whole range of equipment on land, the possibility of walking unaided in the water and swimming independently is a great thrill.

3

Breath control

In any swimming session involving people with disabilities, probably the most frequently heard command is 'Blow'. Why are swimmers asked to blow? How does it increase their learning and enjoyment in the water?

Why breath control is important

The most important reason is safety. Most people, if suddenly immersed in the water, breathe in by instinct. To counteract this danger, swimmers have to be taught to blow every time their face comes near to the water. They should practise this until the reaction is automatic.

How it is taught

This can be done by progressive stages.

- Swimmer's face above water, say blowing a ball.

2 Breath control – blowing poached eggs

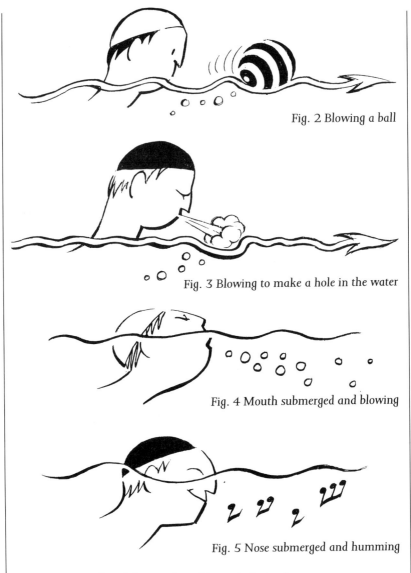

Fig. 2 Blowing a ball

Fig. 3 Blowing to make a hole in the water

Fig. 4 Mouth submerged and blowing

Fig. 5 Nose submerged and humming

- Swimmer's head forward, making a hole in the water.
- Face at water level, blowing sponges or eggs.
- Mouth submerged or partially submerged, oral breathing.
- Nasal breathing ('humming').
- The final test is automatic rhythmical breathing while performing other skills.

Some people with disabilities have difficulty in expanding their chests against the pressure of the water and so inhaling is difficult. If taught to breathe out in a strong, purposeful and deliberate way – in other words, to blow – they will also be able to inhale more easily. This is so because the chest wall muscles recoil like a piece of elastic stretched and let go. Inhaling is a natural reaction to exhaling.

When it is taught

From the outset, start working on breath control. Swimmers are taught to blow out every time their mouth comes near the water so that this response becomes automatic. Control, good timing and rhythm are essential for those who wish to progress to swimming strokes.

Reasons for blowing and not breath holding

Holding the breath is not the way to be safe in water. It increases tension and this in turn increases one's relative density; as a result, one is less buoyant. Holding the breath also causes the build-up of carbon dioxide in the bloodstream; the respiratory centre in the brain will be stimulated to make that person breathe in, even though he may still be submerged. Breathing out by blowing or humming prevents the inhalation of water. All breathing activities should be practised in moderation. This skill may take a long time to learn.

Fig. 6 *The ultimate in breath control*

Details of the association's video 'Breathtaking' can be found on page 126.

4

Entries, exits and helping in the water

From the very first time that you meet it is important that you establish an empathy with a swimmer so that he will want to come back a second time. You need to provide the security that will give him confidence to enter the pool, and you will want to make the experience a happy one. If you fail in these aims your swimmer may not return.

Making eye contact and smiling is a useful start. Learning the correct theory of supporting is absolutely necessary. However, because it is so difficult to describe body positions adequately, it is also essential for instructors to take part in water demonstrations and practice.

Entering the pool

Once you have the confidence of the swimmer, bear in mind that an entry into the water must be safe for both the instructor and swimmer, and that you are working towards the swimmer's eventual independence. For both these reasons swimmers are encouraged to enter the water as follows.

Steps are not recommended. A slip may lead to injury from the poolside or rails. Also, using steps would deprive the swimmers of the tremendous sense of achievement and independence that comes with getting into the water without help.

The instructor selects a depth of water where he can stand safely and comfortably. This depth acts as a cushion for the swimmer as he enters the pool, and will prevent the feet jarring on the pool floor.

In photograph 3 the instructor is in the pool in a well-balanced position, feet apart, knees bent, one foot in front of the other, reaching up with his palms supporting the swimmer around the shoulder blades. The swimmer sits with his palms resting on the instructor's shoulders. Some swimmers may also need extra sitting support from a helper on the poolside.

Remember, this can be a tense moment for a new swimmer. Encouragement, support and eye contact all help. A suggestion to

3   Entry to the water – the first stage, with maximum support around the shoulder blades

4   Entry to the water – hand-on-hand support

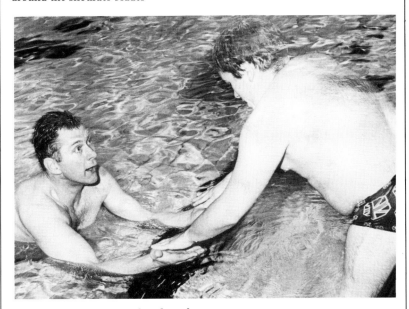

5   Entry to the water – hands and a gap

'Look at me' will ensure that the swimmer keeps his head forwards, and your head will block his possibly frightening view of the vast expanse of water. As the swimmer enters the water, encourage him to blow. This skill must be learned before the swimmer moves on to an independent entry; it's never too early to start practising.

Once a swimmer becomes confident the instructor can progress to supporting him by the elbows as he enters the water. The next step is hand-on-hand support with the instructor's flat upturned palms supporting the swimmer's downturned ones (photographs 4 and 5). Eventually the swimmer may triumphantly enter the water without help. Before the last stage is attempted, though, it is important for the swimmer to have adequate head and breath control.

Some swimmers prefer, while still looking at the instructor, to turn as they fall forwards into the water. There is no risk of them jarring on the pool floor as they will finish the entry in a back float position. The instructor stands with his back to the pool wall, at one side of the swimmer and guides him into the water as he turns, using a 'combined rotation' (see chapter 5).

6   Combined rotational entry –
ready

7   Combined rotational entry –
head turned

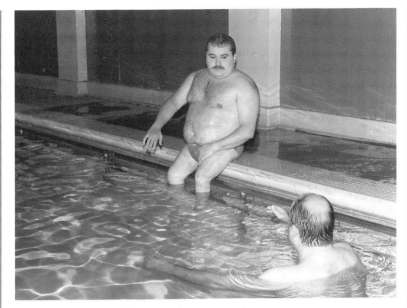

8   Unaided combined rotational entry – ready

9   Unaided combined rotational entry – and he's in

21

Getting out

Safety and eventual independence are again the key factors dictating how the swimmer gets out of the pool.

Vertical or 'wriggle' exit

The swimmer places his hands on the poolside while the instructor assists by guiding at the hips using the rhythm '1,2,3 and up'. The swimmer lifts his chest up and well forwards on to the poolside. Using his hands to help him, the swimmer wriggles forwards until his hips are securely on the poolside. Then he can roll over and sit up.

Horizontal lift

If a swimmer cannot manage the vertical exit he will need more help – three instructors (sometimes more), a bathside helper and a canvas lifting seat at the ready. The instructors select a depth of water that minimises the strain on their backs. The swimmer lies in a back float

10   (above left) Exit from the water – '1, 2, 3 . . . and I'm up', or half way at least

11   (above) Exit from the water – the next stage: 'A few more wriggles and I'll be there'. Note the swimmer's legs are supported if necessary

12   (left) Exit from the water – 'Nearly on far enough to roll over'

13   Horizontal lift – *ready to be lifted*

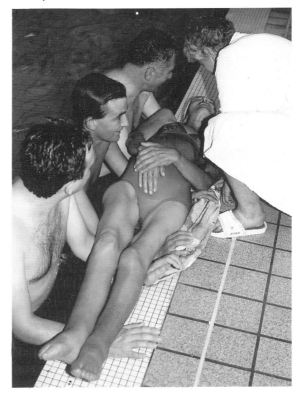

14   Horizontal lift – *safely lifted on to the poolside*

position, parallel to the poolside, with his arms crossed on his chest. The instructors, having decided who will give the lead, stand shoulder to shoulder, the strongest in the middle. They slide their arms, with hands palms down, under the swimmer. One instructor takes care to protect the swimmer's head.

The middle instructor takes the greatest weight and also prevents the swimmer rolling back into the water. Using a smooth, strong rhythm the swimmer is moved up and down in the water to gather momentum, to the call of '1,2,3 and up'. On 'up' the instructors lift up the swimmer to place him on the poolside, aiming his buttocks into the waiting canvas lifting seat. The bathside helper makes sure the swimmer is safe, particularly his head (see the section on moving and assisting in chapter 14). The swimmer is then swivelled round carefully into a sitting position. The instructors must protect his feet as they clear the poolside. Now the swimmer is ready to be lifted in his seat into his wheelchair, again making sure that his feet clear the poolside safely.

This procedure may occasionally be needed in reverse for entry. A swimmer who is not able to sit on the poolside may be rolled into the water.

Instructors should practise these entries and exits on each other until they are proficient, before they start to assist swimmers.

Supporting in the water

A basic aim of AST teaching is to give only as much support as is needed, thus allowing maximum support from the water.

Always support with flat hands and discourage the swimmer from gripping because this increases tension. Initially the support should be firm and the swimmer kept close to the instructor. Gradually, as the swimmer becomes more independent, support can be reduced. Make sure that your hands are always well under the water.

Support the swimmer's trunk but leave his head free. If a swimmer is ever to learn to control his own balance, he will need to have mastered control of his head – the key factor in controlling body balance. This practice must begin right from the start.

Instructors and, when appropriate, also the swimmers, adopt the 'chair' position in the water. Knees are bent and feet are apart, flat on the pool floor as if sitting in a chair. It helps balance to keep the head and arms forwards as if leaning your hands flat on a table.

Vertical supports

Face to face

The swimmer, having entered the water and looking at the instructor, is already in a face-to-face position. The instructor's flat palms offer support at the trunk, elbows or hand-on-hand, as needed.

Fig. 7 Face-to-face position with eye contact

Occasionally the swimmer may need to sit straddled across the instructor with the instructor's hands supporting from behind.

Instructor behind the swimmer

Both instructor and swimmer adopt the chair position, with the instructor behind the swimmer, supporting his trunk. The swimmer uses his head and arms to balance himself as he does his activities.

To provide the security for a swimmer who needs much more support, especially if his feet are off the pool floor, the instructor puts his arms forwards between the swimmer's elbows and body, flat palms upturned as in the face-to-face support. The palms can then be

15 Instructor
supporting from
behind the
swimmer

raised if the swimmer falls forwards and the instructor's chest can be pressed forwards to restore the swimmer's balance if he falls back.

Horizontal supports

From the chair position, with the instructor's hands on the swimmer's pelvis, the swimmer can put his head back so his ears are in the water, and then let his feet float to the surface. Allowing the water to support the swimmer's head enables the swimmer to control his own head movements.

When the swimmer is working on lateral rotation which involves rolling from side to side (*see* chapter 5), the instructor may support from the side by facing the swimmer with his shoulders out of the water (for once) and one hand on each side of the swimmer's hips.

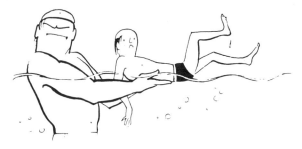

Fig. 8 *Frequent error of new helpers! Allow your swimmer to float naturally with minimum support*

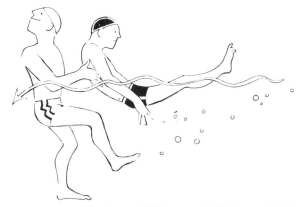

Fig. 9 *Incorrect handling means the swimmer is unable to appreciate the support of the water*

Supports in group formation

These supports may be used in a circle or in a line for both vertical and horizontal positions. One extra instructor is needed for the end of a line.

Short-arm support

The instructor tucks his arms between the swimmer's elbows and body, his flat upturned palms to his swimmer's downturned ones. When he wants to reduce support to give the swimmer greater freedom, the instructor slides his elbows under and to the outside of the swimmer's elbows.

Long-arm support

Swimmers are supported palm to palm, but this time both the instructor and swimmer have their arms extended. Swimmers will need to have developed reasonable head control before they work in this position.

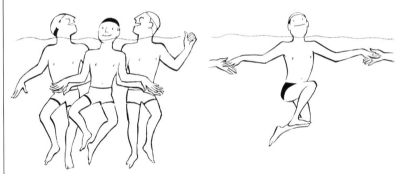

Fig. 10 Short-arm support   Fig. 11 Long-arm support

Cross-arm support

This vertical support in a circle is useful for swimmers who have poor vertical control. The instructors on each side of the swimmer pass their arm which is nearest to the swimmer across his back to hold the opposite hip. By keeping close to the swimmer they can give as much support as they need to.

With practice the instructor will learn to change smoothly from one support to another, as changes in activity demand different

16   Cross-arm
support

degrees or methods of support. On occasion, an instructor will have to use two different supports at the same time if a swimmer on one side of him needs a different kind of help to the one on the other side.

When working in group formation it is especially important to take care that swimmers on either side of an instructor are not compromised in their balance by poor or lop-sided support.

17   *File formation*

File formation

To work in this formation each person places his hands round the hips of the person in front. If a swimmer needs more support than this gives, the instructor, with the swimmer in front of him, should place his arms between the swimmer's arms and body, and put his own hands securely rounds the hips of the instructor in front.

Change of formation

To allow the lesson to flow easily, instructors should be able to change from one formation to another with little interruption. For example: (I=instructor, S=swimmer)

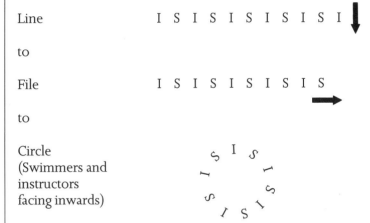

Line	I S I S I S I S I S I ↓
to	
File	I S I S I S I S I S
	→
to	
Circle (Swimmers and instructors facing inwards)	

(Arrows depict direction in which instructors and swimmers are facing.)

   Don't be disheartened if progress seems slow. Some of the progressions in support described here may take considerable time, possibly even years, to achieve with some swimmers.

5

Rotations

A relaxed swimmer's body floating in water will tend to take up a very stable position. The only problem here is that the swimmer's face may be under the water. To achieve a safe breathing position, the swimmer has to turn or rotate. From chapter 9 we will discover that forces in line produce no rotation, and so to produce a rotation the swimmer must move his centre of gravity (that is, change his weight distribution) or his centre of buoyancy (change his shape under the water). As a change, or asymmetry, in the shape of the body will create a roll, it is obvious that a swimmer with a physical disability that alters a 'normal' balanced shape will have a tendency to roll.

In practice, there are three forms of rotation that are useful: vertical, lateral and, using part of both of these, the combined rotation. Although they are described in this order, their teaching usually follows the pattern of vertical, combined, lateral and then more advanced rotations (i.e. somersaults). This is because the combined rotation introduces the lateral roll and also provides a safety measure in that the swimmer learns a method of attaining a safe breathing position should he fall into the water.

When asked to perform rotations in the water, most people will carry them out at such a rate that they are unable to describe how they were performed. It must be stressed that in teaching these rotations, they should, after initiation by the swimmer, be carried out at the speed that the water will allow, and if necessary completed with help from the instructor. The roll consists of about 25% initiation and maintaining shape, 50% passive roll, 25% recovery. It is the water that does the turning. The swimmer merely changes shape and waits for the roll to occur.

Vertical rotation

Vertical rotation is an early skill needed to allow the swimmer to lie back in the water and then regain the vertical position.

The swimmer is taught to attain a back float by moving his head back (chin tucked in). As he does so, his feet will move forwards and rise to the surface. The swimmer then brings his head forwards and reaches with his arms, slowly but continuously (*see* photographs 18 and 19). He will find that his feet sink to the floor. If at the same time he brings his knees up to his chin, he will find that in this 'ball' shape it takes much less effort to rotate than in a longer 'stick' position. Remember, the swimmer should be encouraged to breathe out as the face comes near the water. The instructor only needs to help the swimmer balance, resisting the great temptation to push the swimmer forwards during the recovery.

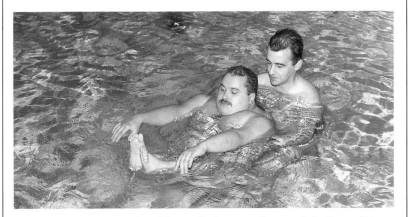

18   *Vertical rotation – head forwards, keep reaching and the feet will eventually sink*

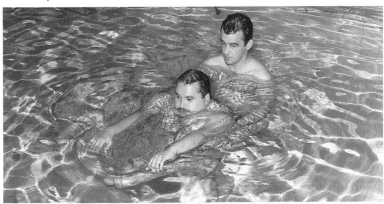

19   *Vertical rotation – success!*

The ultimate vertical rotation is a somersault, either forwards or backwards. This essential skill proves the swimmer's ability to return to a safe breathing position from any position in the water, whether he is in that position through choice or accident. (Teaching somersaults is clearly demonstrated in the 'Breathtaking' video – *see* p.126).

The mushroom float introduces the swimmer to a rotation where his face is submerged. With the swimmer 'sitting in his chair', he is encouraged to tuck his chin in and then to bring his knees up to his chin while supported by the instructor. The swimmer then clasps his shins and keeps his head forwards. With a controlled rotation the instructor allows the swimmer to roll forwards while telling him to hum, thus preventing the water going up his nose. Eventually the swimmer takes up his position himself with no support and is happy to be twisted and turned in all directions knowing that he will always return to this position (*see* photographs in chapter 6).

Lateral rotation

This rotation is like a rolling log in water and is sometimes called 'horizontal'. It is a rotation around the spine and may take place in an upright or horizontal position. Since many people with a physical disability have a tendency to roll, the first stage in teaching the lateral rotation is to teach the ability to correct an unwanted one.

In an activity known as 'Don't let me roll you' (*see* photograph 20) the instructor takes up a position to one side of the floating swimmer

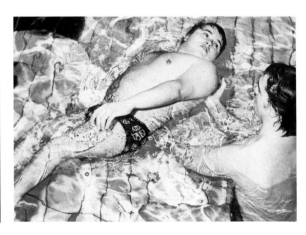

20 *Lateral rotation* – 'Don't let me roll you'

and at shoulder level. By placing one hand under the nearest shoulder of the swimmer, he attempts to roll the swimmer slowly away from himself, the other hand being used for support. The swimmer must turn his head towards the raised shoulder, eventually looking over his shoulder as his body is turned more. By developing the skill of turning his head, the swimmer can counteract the rotation to achieve a stable position in the water. The anti-rotating effect can be enhanced by crossing the leg and arm furthest from the turning force over the mid-line of the body. This skill should be practised in both directions. Using these principles the swimmer can learn to initiate a controlled lateral rotation.

The instructor stands to one side of the swimmer, supporting him at hip level with one hand over the swimmer and one underneath. The swimmer can then use any combination of the following to produce a roll towards the helper (*see* photograph 21): turning his head towards the helper; crossing the far arm and/or leg across the mid-line; or twisting the hips.

These actions should be enough to produce a three-quarter roll with little effort. If there is no turning effect, the instructor must check that a turning effect due, say, to the head, is not unwittingly being self-corrected by the swimmer twisting his hips in the opposite direction or extending the near arm. At about three-quarters of the way through the roll, many swimmers will have lost momentum and the roll will tend to 'stick'. This is the time, and not before, for the instructor to help complete the roll, if necessary by taking hold of the hips and guiding the swimmer on to his back (*see* photograph 22).

21   *Lateral rotation — beginning a full rotation*

22 *Lateral rotation — a little help at the hips at the half-way stage*

23 *Lateral rotation — 'You can do this alone but I'm here just in case'*

24 *Lateral rotation — unaided*

A half roll should be practised every time a back float activity comes to the side of the pool. On approach, the swimmer looks to the side in the direction that he is going to roll. By continuing to look at the side, a roll is initiated that can be easily completed by using the upper arm to take hold of the side. The swimmer's arm takes the 'long way round' (see photograph 23). The instructor must ensure he does not get in the way.

25   Combined rotation – this is the right way to come to the poolside

26   Combined rotation – safely there

Combined rotation

The combined rotation, as its name suggests, is a combination of the previously described skills.

When the swimmer is standing up from a back float position, the instructor should be directly behind. If the swimmer should over-reach in this position, he comes directly up against the instructor's thighs and hips and so he cannot fall forwards. If, for some reason, the instructor is not in this position, the swimmer may fall on to his face. At this stage there is no point in trying to heave the swimmer backwards. The instructor rolls the swimmer from the hips to re-store a safe breathing position, and allows him to attempt to start again.

27 Combined rotation – ready to practise an unaided combined rotation

28 Combined rotation – turning the head

29 Combined rotation – achieving a back float position

30   *Combined rotation – completed by a forward rotation*

This activity can be practised by having the swimmer stand up then fall forwards. The instructor, who is standing to one side of the swimmer, then asks the swimmer to look at him. Turning the head will automatically result in the shoulders following and the combined rotation is half completed before the swimmer's face is completely under water.

The upright position can be regained with a further vertical rotation.

Competence and elegance in rotations are at the core of being water free. Rotations should be mastered and then continually practised, for although it is possible to swim without control of rotation, it is not possible to be safe.

6

Buoyancy and upthrust

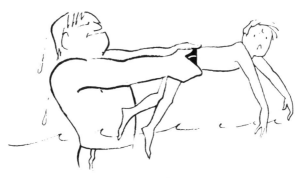

Fig. 12 How **not** to do it: let the water do the supporting

Most people float in water. Buoyancy is the property a body has which enables it to float: upthrust is the force that the water applies to that body.

Confidence comes from understanding what will happen as a result of certain actions and circumstances. In swimming the belief that the force of upthrust is always acting and will make a body float is probably as close to what people call confidence as one can reach.

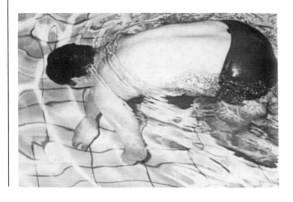

31 Upthrust – an instructor demonstrating upthrust by trying to crawl along the floor of the pool

Upthrust can be felt if you try to crawl on your hands and knees under water. It is impossible to keep your hands and knees on the bottom as a strong force of upthrust pushes you towards the surface.

A mushroom float (*see* photograph 32) is created by curling up into a ball with the head tucked in and the arms wrapped around your knees. The natural floating position is with the back upper-most, just breaking the surface. If an instructor pushes a swimmer to the bottom, upthrust will always return him to the surface, eventually to the same position.

Try to sit on the bottom of the pool in chest-deep water. You will need a very determined effort to get down.

With experience comes confidence, so we relax more. Our bodies are less dense and upthrust is more effective (*see* chapter 9).

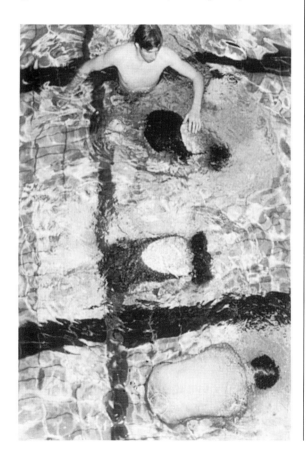

32 Mushroom floats. *All three swimmers have been pushed down, now they are bobbing up – that's upthrust*

7

Balance

What do we understand by 'balance'? Most people will have acquired a sense of balance long before they learned the word. Balance is an ability to know that in given positions or activities you can remain still when you need to (static balance), or create controlled patterns of movement and afterwards return to stillness in a selected posture (dynamic balance).

Rolling, sitting, kneeling, crawling, standing, walking, jumping, running and climbing all require balance in varying degrees. We progress from one skill to the next using what we have learnt previously. Once we have learnt to control our bodies, we proceed to learn skills involving an inanimate object – for example, ball throwing and kicking, using a bat or racket, or riding a bike.

We adjust our balance by moving our head, trunk and arms until our sense of balance tells us that we are in a state of equilibrium. If, due to disability, a swimmer has not had the experience on land to acquire these skills, or through illness or accident some abilities have been impaired, the swimmer may find it hard to learn to balance.

Balancing in the water

We are concerned with balance in the water. With the help of the instructor who tries to analyse how balance can be achieved, and with the support of the water, first static balance and then dynamic balance can be taught or retaught.

As long as a swimmer can touch the bottom or side of the pool there is an 'on land' pattern of recognition and a sense of familiarity. The swimmer can exert a force against the bottom and stand up or pull himself to the side. He can learn many aspects of balance at this level and feel safe and relaxed. Breathing is easy to control, allowing a good supply of air to the lungs, and oxygen to the brain; there is no tension.

When, however, there is nothing to lean or push against, there are swimmers who will become fearful and distressed – the familiar has been removed. A person who lacks spatial perception may feel totally disorientated if he cannot see a limb or feel it in contact with a known object. He may become tense, be unable to control his breathing, and try to reach out and touch something for reassurance.

Some people with no sensitivity in their legs may feel totally insecure and become quickly distressed if they are turned on to their backs in a floating position.

Tension, fear, insecurity and disorientation, which are often associated with shallow breathing, can all make the swimmer less buoyant and can confuse patterns of movement and control.

An instructor must understand his role when taking a swimmer through the first phases of being totally water supported: correct support, clear communication and gradual disengagement at the optimum time are essential.

To be balanced in the water one does not have to be absolutely still. An experienced swimmer, when floating in rough water, is continually adjusting his balance, creating chosen patterns of movement within his physical ability, swimming, rolling or submerging while maintaining a safe breathing position. He is mentally and physically balanced.

Floating

To be competent in water, swimmers should learn to balance in the vertical position, on their backs, on their fronts, and to adjust their balance to accommodate breathing.

The vertical float

This is often the most difficult to learn, especially for anyone with poorly developed lower limbs and a powerful torso. (See fig. 38, p.59.)

On the back

It is possible for most of the body to be immersed with just the face being clear of the water to allow easy breathing. Posture is critical. If the head is taken back too far, making the arch of the spine concave, the feet and head will sink. Conversely, if the head is lifted too high, its weight, no longer supported by the water, will cause the head and shoulders to sink. The correct position is to have the ears in the water, chin tucked down on to the chest, and eyes looking along the body to the toes (*see* photograph 1, p.10).

On the front

Being face down presents obvious breathing problems. It is necessary, therefore, that a swimmer must have learnt breath control before he tries to learn face-down strokes.

Swimming strokes

Gliding from the side, breathing out into the water, maintaining good posture throughout the glide, and keeping in a straight and horizontal line, are all exercises in balance. From this it is a natural progression to learn arm and leg movements and to co-ordinate breathing.

Remember, balance control is the key to all structured activity. The more structured the activity, the greater the skill needed to control balance.

8

Movement through the water

Fig. 13 Turbulence: the mother duck draws her brood along in her wake

For the keen new swimmer, being able to swim on his own is often the first goal, but one of the last to be achieved. The swimmer must first go through various stages of adjustment to water, such as breath control, rotations, and gaining the confidence that comes from realising that water offers great support through upthrust.

Independence in the water

An instructor can make clear to a swimmer from a very early stage that self-initiated movement through water starts long before independent swimming. Being aware of this is important in giving a swimmer a feeling of achievement.

A basic rotation, for instance, triggered by the controlled movement of the head, is a self-initiated movement through water, as is walking, bicycling and kangaroo jumping. They can all be part of the build-up to horizontal propulsion.

The term 'propulsion' is used rather than 'swimming' because the latter suggests one of the four main swimming strokes. Swimming is defined as *progression at, or below, the surface of the water by working the arms, legs or body*. The action of the head is also an important part of swimming because it acts as a corrective in balance control.

The back float is the ideal position from which to start horizontal movement. It is a good balanced position in which breath control is easy. The same cannot be said when the swimmer is facing downwards: any attempt to take a breath will disturb the balance. Holding the head up out of the water in this position is no solution because it inevitably results in increased tension.

Turbulent gliding

Fig. 14 Turbulent gliding: the balanced swimmer moves in the turbulence created by the instructor

Turbulent gliding is the movement through the water which results from the instructor using turbulence to draw the swimmer along without any physical contact. The swimmer takes up a back float position and only needs to make small contra-rotational movements to maintain his balance while appreciating the feeling of moving through the water. Some support may be needed at the swimmer's centre of balance at first to initiate the movement. Once the swimmer is correctly balanced this can be withdrawn.

The instructor then moves slowly backwards through the water. This creates the turbulence that will draw the swimmer with him in the same way as ducklings are drawn after their mother. Further turbulence can be created by the instructor's hands moving rhythmically beneath the swimmer's shoulder blades as he moves back.

To keep moving in a straight line, the instructor has to position himself correctly behind the swimmer's head and create the turbulence centrally. He must also make sure that he is neither too close nor so far away that the turbulence is ineffectual.

Frequently, this is the swimmer's first experience of sustained un-

33 Turbulent gliding – *note the turbulence between helper and swimmer*

supported movement through the water. He may be anxious at the thought of being completely independent while he's learning a new skill. A little mild cunning might help to persuade your swimmer to accept that he can manage being on his own.

In the end total disengagement can only come about as a result of utter trust between swimmer and helper. Allow enough time to build up complete confidence.

The first strokes

After turbulent gliding, the next stage is for the swimmer to make some movements to achieve progress. Ideally, the first movements should be close to the swimmer's centre of balance so as to minimise the upset to that balance.

The method of movement will depend on the swimmer's ability.

Fig. 15 Sculling: the first stage of independent propulsion

45

Where possible, a sculling type action is used. This can be taught, in the first place, by asking the swimmer to 'Clap your sides'. This can lead on to a hand movement where the hands, palm downwards, are moved to and from the body at the level of the hips, rather like the pectoral fins of a fish. Movement here is quite slow and the swimmer must be told that it should be so.

Once the sculling has been mastered, leg or further arm action can start. It is important for the instructor to assess the swimmer's capabilities accurately so that he can decide whether a leg or an arm action will generate the most efficient propulsion. Teaching one or the other, instead of both, is advisable at first because co-ordination, balance and control are facilitated when the movement is confined to either lower or upper limbs. It is also easier to spot and correct faults.

The arm action

The arm action begins as an extended sculling action with both arms together. It is then developed until the arms can be raised just out of the water and taken to the level of the shoulders. Lifting the arms high out of the water would lead to the body sinking. Besides, the increase in power and pull would not be of any great benefit to the novice swimmer.

When the arms are at shoulder level they are put back into the water and, kept straight, pulled back to the side of the body. The cycle is then repeated.

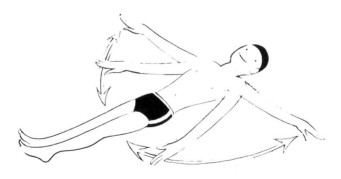

Fig. 16 The next stage after sculling

The leg action

Leg action should stem from the hips and use a straight, slow kick. The main kicking faults are bending the legs too much, 'thrashing', and allowing the hips to fall to a lower level so that the body is bent almost at a right angle. A bad leg action, with bent knees, can result in turbulence which produces movement downwards and even backwards. The first two faults can often be corrected by constant reminders to straighten the legs or slow down the kick rate. Where the hips are sinking, the swimmer must be told to raise them by pushing the stomach up without arching the back.

Once the separate arm and leg actions have been mastered, the two can be combined, if this is possible. It is then up to the swimmer, under the guidance of the instructor, to decide whether to concentrate on the arms or the legs for the main propulsive force.

Stroke style

Although we initially teach swimming on the back, swimming on the side or front are good additional styles, once the swimmer has good breath control and is confident. Swimmers should be encouraged to change from one stroke to another.

Swimmers who, because of their disability, have a tendency to veer to one side, may find that altering the position of the head to the side will allow them to swim in a straight line.

It is useful for clubs to have someone who is capable of analysing a swimmer's method in order to reduce any inefficient action and to allow full development of potential.

9

Effects of water

Fig. 17 *Have you ever thought?*

While it is possible to be an adequate instructor without much knowledge of the effects of water, instructors will eventually find themselves limited unless they learn to understand the action and interaction of water on a body that is immersed, according to the laws of physics. These laws govern all we do in the water.

Water is different from air

There are many differences between our everyday world of air and solid surfaces, and the world of water. Some are straightforward: water is wet, air is not; we can feel water, we do not usually feel air; we can breathe in and out in air, but when our face is in water we must not breathe in.

Two other phenomena become noticeable on entering the water. Firstly, movement is slowed down: try clapping your hands in the air, then under the water. Many of the movements that are easy to perform in the air can be made only slowly in water. Secondly, you become aware of an upthrust or lifting force – usually called 'buoyancy' – as you go deeper into the water.

Not only is it difficult to move fast in water, but it is also difficult to stop moving or to change direction. Try walking for ten paces or so

Fig. 18 *Air is much less dense than water*

Fig. 19 *Water is much more dense than air*

in water that is chest deep, then turn around and walk back: the first few returning steps are very hard going. This is because the water, which is 800 times more dense than air, is now moving. Walking back is like walking upstream in a flowing river.

So, being in water is vastly different from being in air. We must re-learn how to balance, turn, lie down, get up, and so on, because the methods of doing these will be different. Many of our ways of doing things on dry land will let us down when we are in the water. With skilled teaching, however, these differences can be turned to great advantage.

Terminology

To understand basic physical principals, some frequently-used terms need to be understood.

Volume

Volume means the space that the body occupies. A person who needs a size 16 track suit has a greater volume than someone who needs a size 12.

Mass and weight

Mass and weight are often thought to be terms that are directly interchangeable. But weight is the effect of gravity acting on a body, while mass is the quantity of matter in a body. A body on the moon will weigh less than on earth, whereas its mass will remain constant. If you find the concept of 'mass' difficult to understand, thinking of weight may help. Someone who weighs more on the bathroom scales has a greater mass than someone who weighs less.

Density

Most people have been asked whether it is a pound of lead or a pound of feathers that is heavier. While we know that they weigh the same, everyone is tempted to say that lead is heavier, and generally the statement that lead is heavy is not regarded as silly. Even so, half a pound of lead is clearly only half the weight of a pound of feathers. The significant property here is the volume in relation to the mass.

Fig. 20 Which is heavier, a pound of lead or a pound of feathers? Of course, they weigh the same. But we are at first tempted to say the lead because it is more dense than feathers

When we say that lead is heavier, we are usually thinking of equal volumes of lead and feathers.

The volume of a pound of feathers is far greater than the volume of a pound of lead. The relationship between volume and mass is known as density. Lead has a greater density than feathers and this is what we really mean when we say that lead is heavier. Density is usually measured in units of grams per cubic centimetre.

$$\text{Density} = \text{mass of body} \div \text{volume of body}$$

Pure water, at a temperature of 4° C, has a density of 1g/cc. This is a useful figure with which to make comparisons with the density of other materials. We call this ratio of the density of the material to the density of water 'relative density'. An object weighing 10g with 1cc volume will have a relative density of 10; a body weighing 100g of 50cc volume will have a relative density of 2.

$$\text{Relative density} = \text{density of body} \div \text{density of water}$$

Relative density also tells us the ratio of the mass of the substance to the mass of an equal volume of water. If we have 1cc of water and 1cc of a particular piece of wood, the water will weigh 1g and the wood, say, 0.75g. The relative density of this piece of wood will be three-quarters that of the water.

Floating and sinking

Many people claim that they do not float: usually they are wrong because surprisingly few people cannot float. Floating is dependent on relative density.

Anything with a relative density greater than 1.0 (i.e. more dense than water) will sink; anything with a relative density less than 1.0 (i.e. less dense than water) will float. The overall relative density of the human body is determined by the relative proportions of bone, muscle, fat, etc, and the amount of air in the lungs.

Human bodies are generally in the range of 0.93 − 1.0 relative density (very few are over 1.0). This means that most people float, but only just, since their relative density is close to 1.0.

To help understand floating we need to consider the two forces of gravity and buoyancy. For a stationary (not rotating) float these forces have to be equal and opposite, and vertically in line.

Fig. 21 Most of us float, but only just – our relative density is close to 1.0

What is a force?

Most of us understand 'force' to be associated with movement or change. A force acting on a stationary object can cause it to start moving, but if the object is already moving it will speed up, slow down, stop or change direction depending on the direction and strength of the force.

If a man pushes a car along a flat road, he is applying a force in order to make it move. It will continue to move after he has stopped pushing but will slow down and eventually stop because of opposing forces. Whenever a body is seen to change direction, slow down or speed up, this change is caused by a force. In water, the slowing down and stopping occurs because of the 'impedance' of the water (*see* p.66).

Reasons for rotating in the water

Forces in line

In water, we need to consider whether or not the two forces – gravity and buoyancy – are acting in line.

Gravity/buoyancy

Gravity is the force by which a body is pulled down to the earth; buoyancy is the force that provides upthrust.

Forces in line either cause movement in a straight line or cause a state of rest. If the forces are equal and opposite, no movement

Fig. 22 No movement

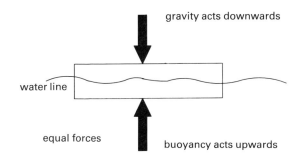

Fig. 23 Object floating

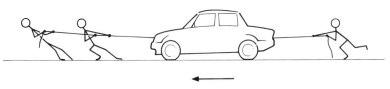

Fig. 24 Movement

occurs. If the forces are unequal and opposite, movement will occur in the direction of the greater force.

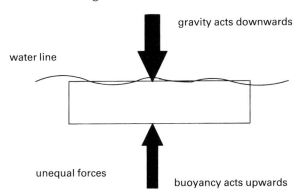

Fig. 25 Object sinking

Centre of gravity

When you go to pick up a large object, you usually lift it in the middle. If it tips one way, you put it down and pick it up nearer to the end that was tipping down. This balance point that you are trying to find is the centre of gravity. The centre of gravity is the point through which the force of gravity acts.

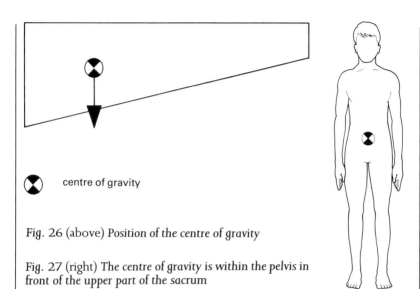

centre of gravity

Fig. 26 (above) *Position of the centre of gravity*

Fig. 27 (right) *The centre of gravity is within the pelvis in front of the upper part of the sacrum*

The centre of gravity of the human body varies according to build, sex, age, and shape. Someone with very dense legs, for example, will have a lower centre of gravity. We cannot change our bodies, at least in the short term, but we can change our shape. Raising our arms above our head will raise our centre of gravity.

Centre of buoyancy

The centre of buoyancy is the centre of the volume of the water that is displaced when a body is immersed. It is the point through which the buoyancy force acts. With a floating human body it is the centre of the volume of the part that is submerged (i.e. the centre of water displaced).

For an object to float motionless, the forces of buoyancy and gravity must be equal and opposite.

When an object is wholly or partially immersed in water, it displaces a volume of water equivalent to the volume of the object that is immersed. Add a lump of ice to a drink and you will see the level rise in the glass.

The water that is displaced when the object is immersed has a weight and will try to push the object upwards out of the water. This upward force is known as 'buoyancy' and will determine whether the object will sink or float.

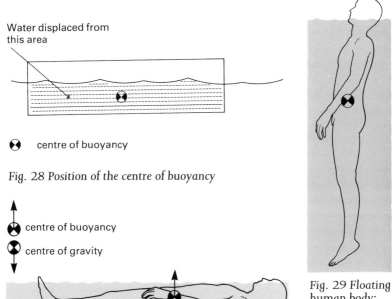

Water displaced from this area

⊗ centre of buoyancy

Fig. 28 Position of the centre of buoyancy

⊕ centre of buoyancy

⊗ centre of gravity

Fig. 30 When the forces of buoyancy and gravity are equal and opposite, an object will float motionless

Fig. 29 Floating human body: centre of buoyancy is centre of volume of part submerged

If the object is more dense than water it will sink, displacing the equivalent of its own volume. Since the weight of water displaced is less than the weight of the object, it does not provide sufficient buoyancy for floating to occur. (See fig. 32.)

An object less dense than water will displace a volume of water equal to the part of it that is immersed. While the volume of this displaced water is equal to the volume of the submerged part, its weight is equal to the weight of the whole object. This provides sufficient buoyancy for the object to float. (See fig. 31.)

The density of an object determines not only if it will float, but how well it will float (how buoyant it is). By studying the relative density of objects we can tell how well they are going to float. A particular piece of wood with a relative density of 0.75 will float with 25% above water. Cork, with a relative density of 0.22, will float with 78% above water. (See fig. 33.)

A study of different parts of the body will reveal that some have a relative density greater than 1.0 (i.e. they would sink), while others are less than 1.0 (i.e. would float):

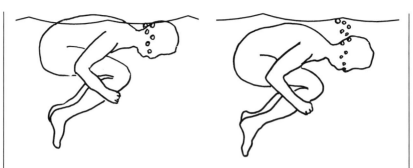

Fig. 31 Mushroom float   Fig. 32 Attempted mushroom float

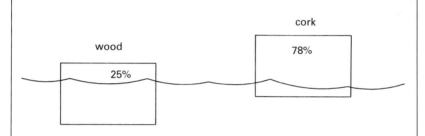

Fig. 33 The block of wood, with a relative density of 0.75, will float with 25% above water. The cork, with a relative density of 0.22, will float with 78% above water

air (found in cavities, e.g. the chest)	0.00125
body fat	0.942
muscle	1.158
rib bone	1.383
tooth	2.240

On average, the relative density of the human body is 0.95, so we float with 5% of our body above the water surface. A person with a large amount of body fat will float more easily than a more muscular person.

Fig. 34 A person with a large amount of body fat (right) will float more easily than a more muscular person (left)

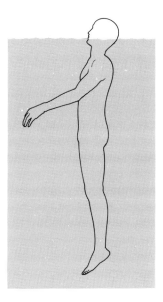

Fig. 35 Vertical float

When a person first starts to learn to float, it is important that the part that is out of the water includes the airways. Therefore, every effort must be made to keep the rest of the body below the surface.

Some people feel they cannot float. To find out if they can, ask them to perform a mushroom float. They must have good mental adjustment to water and sufficient breath control to try this. Wait and see what happens . . . most people float at the surface with a small area of their back out of the water. By changing their body shape they can find a different floating position with the mouth and/or nose out of the water, for example a vertical float.

Forces out of line

Take a ruler and lay it on a table. Push it sideways along the table with one finger so that the line of the push passes through its centre of gravity. If you get it just right the ruler will slide without turning. Now move your finger a little to the right and push. The ruler will turn. The rotational effect is the same if a push is applied on either side of the ruler, providing that the fingers are not opposite each other (i.e. they must be out of line). Wherever there is turning or a tendency to turn, forces 'out of line' are at work. This turning is called 'rotation' and is very important in water.

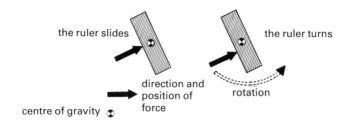

Fig. 36 Forces which are not in line cause turning until they are in line

Having discovered why objects rotate, we need to know how far they rotate. What will happen when forces are applied continuously? This can be shown by using the ruler again. Hold each end between thumb and forefinger, with one hand above the other and the ruler upright. Moving the hands outwards will cause the ruler to rotate and it will turn until it is in line with the pull; in other words, until the forces out of line causing rotation are in line again. Rotation, then, will continue until the out-of-line forces are no longer out of line.

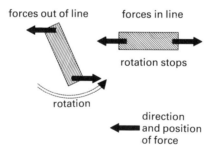

Fig. 37 Rotation continues until the out-of-line forces are no longer out of line

Some people can float easily on their backs. This is because their centre of gravity in such a position is vertically in line with the centre of buoyancy, i.e. the buoyancy force is vertically in line with the gravity force. Mobility in water depends on the swimmer's ability to move the forces of gravity and buoyancy in or out of line, to control or create rotation.

If a swimmer with muscular, dense legs tries to float in a horizontal position, his buoyancy and gravity will be out of line. Rotation will occur and the swimmer will float in a vertical position in which the centres of buoyancy and gravity are vertically in line.

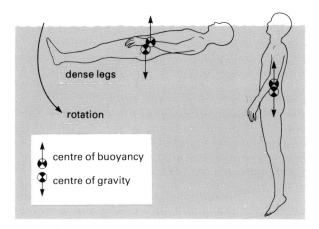

Fig. 38 This swimmer has muscular, dense legs. His horizontal float position cannot be maintained because his centres of buoyancy and gravity are vertically out of line. He will rotate into a vertical float position where the centres of buoyancy and gravity are vertically in line

Fig. 39a The swimmer with muscular, dense legs has a centre of gravity that is low, i.e. towards the feet

Fig. 39b The solution is to change the centre of gravity, either by extending the arms above the head . . .

Fig. 39c . . . or by bending the knees

For such a swimmer to float horizontally, the problem may be solved by changing his centre of gravity by extending the arms above the head, or bending the knees. By changing the shape, a swimmer can stop a rotation and achieve a balanced position.

When supporting a swimmer to help him balance in water, the instructor is trying to help him to learn to keep the centre of gravity vertically in line with the centre of buoyancy. A swimmer can also cause a rotation by changing his shape so that the forces are out of line: floating on his back, he can gain an upright position by tilting his head forwards and reaching forwards with his arms.

The changes in shape needed to stop or cause a rotation can be very small, so even people with limited mobility can learn to control or create movement.

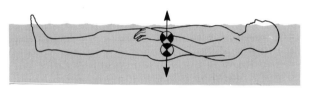

Fig. 40a The swimmer is floating on his back with forces in line

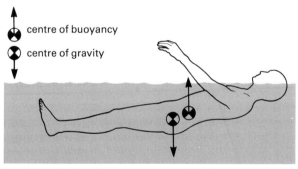

Fig. 40b By tilting the head forwards and reaching forwards with the arms, the swimmer moves the forces out of line and achieves an upright position

Metacentre

If a swimmer is floating in a balanced position and a rotation is caused by an external force such as rough water, the swimmer will either stop rotating one way and then rotate back to the original position (said to be stable), or will continue rotating until a new balanced position is attained (unstable).

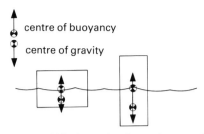

Fig. 41 *Wood blocks with relative density of 0.5*

To help instructor and swimmer to remain stable we need to look at the principle of metacentre. This involves the relationship between the centre of gravity and the centre of buoyancy. Let us compare the two blocks of wood in fig. 41. They weigh the same and are made of the same material but their shape is different. They will both float with half their volume submerged. When gravity and buoyancy forces are in line there is no rotation. If the water is disturbed the blocks will be moved out of balance and will behave differently from each other. Their centres of gravity are fixed points within the body; moving the body does not change their position. What does change is the shape of the displaced water and therefore the centre of buoyancy: the out of line forces cause different effects.

To determine which way the blocks will roll, a pointer needs to be attached to each block. This is like the mast on a ship and passes through its centre of gravity. As the block rolls, so does the mast. A

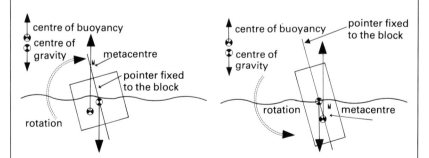

Fig. 42 This block will roll upright again, as the metacentre is above the centre of gravity

Fig. 43 As soon as this block starts to rotate, the new centre of buoyancy causes the metacentre to fall below the centre of gravity. This block is unstable and will rotate until it reaches a new balanced position

vertical line drawn through the centre of buoyancy will meet the pointer at the place marked 'M' in fig. 42. This point is the metacentre.

If the metacentre is *above* the centre of gravity, a body will return to its original position. If the metacentre is *below* the centre of gravity, the body will rotate to a new position.

What happens if the centre of gravity is moved? Look at the man in the canoe in fig. 44.

With the man sitting, the canoe is balanced and quite stable (fig. 44a). By standing up he raises his centre of gravity (fig. 44b). He and the canoe still weigh the same and therefore displace the same amount of water, and the forces are still in line. The canoe is still balanced but it is now unstable. A small force will cause the canoe to tip over and rotate to a new balanced position (fig. 45).

To remain in a balanced and stable position in the water, the centre of gravity must be kept as low as possible so that the

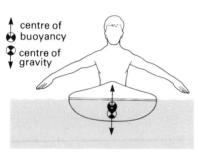

Fig. 44a (left) *The canoe is balanced and stable when the man is sitting*

Fig. 44b (below left) *As he stands up, his centre of gravity is raised. The canoe is still balanced because the forces are still in line, but it is now less stable*

Fig. 45 (below) *A small force will cause the canoe to tip over and rotate to a new balanced position*

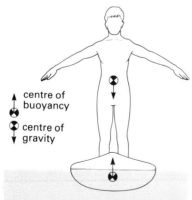

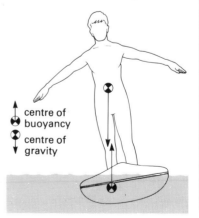

metacentre does not fall below the centre of gravity. Conversely, the metacentric effect can be used to initiate a rotation. The stability of the chair position (*see* page 24) demonstrates the use of the metacentric principle – the centre of gravity is kept low.

Pressure

One of the properties of water is that it will exert pressure on an object immersed in it. This pressure is exerted on all surfaces of the object and increases with depth.

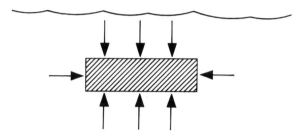

Fig. 46 *The pressure on an object immersed in water is exerted on all surfaces and increases with depth*

Swimmers with a reduced vital lung capacity may find it more difficult to breathe in when they are in the vertical position, with their chest completely under water.

Some ear and eye conditions may prohibit the swimmer from underwater work, because of the risk of problems from the increased pressure. This may also apply to swimmers with shunts (*see* page 102). In fact, extra care should be taken by *all* those who go down to any depth in the water – an increase in pressure may harm the ears.

Turbulence

So far we have looked at the effects of undisturbed water, but how does moving water affect an object immersed in it? This moving or disturbed water is referred to as being 'turbulent'. Turbulent water exerts less pressure on an object immersed in it than still water and therefore the buoyancy is reduced.

In a fluid, a difference of pressure will cause movement of the fluid from the higher to the lower pressure area.

High   Movement   Low

Pressure   Pressure

Fig. 47 Difference in pressure will cause movement from the higher to the lower pressure area

If something is immersed in the fluid, it will also move from the high to the low pressure area.

This is true of air too. Wind is air moving from a high to a low

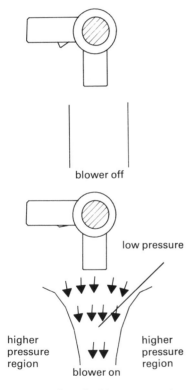

blower off

low pressure

higher pressure region   higher pressure region

blower on

Fig. 48 When the blower is on, the flow of air between the sheets creates a lower pressure area, with higher pressure on the outsides where the air is not being moved: this causes the papers to move together

34   Turbulence – try it; it works

pressure area. This effect can be demonstrated by blowing down between two sheets of A4 paper, held by their top edges about 7cm (3in) apart.

The flow of air down the middle creates a lower pressure area, with higher pressure on the outsides where the air is not being moved. This causes the papers to move together.

We have all experienced the feeling, when standing close to the kerb, of being drawn towards a large passing vehicle – an effect of turbulence. In the same way, an object immersed in water will be moved towards a lower pressure area.

Turbulence works in all directions – up, down, sideways and along the surface of the water.

A person walking backwards creates a slipstream (an area of turbulent water) in front of him. If he drops an object such as a sponge into this area and keeps walking backwards, the object will move with him. Instructors need to bear this in mind when testing a swimmer for the distance they can blow an object, and should stay behind the swimmer so as not to draw the object in their slipstream.

Similarly, in a race or when testing for a distance award, any accompanying instructor should be behind the swimmer.

Turbulent gliding permits swimmers to experience movement through water due to the turbulence created by an instructor (see p.44).

Creating turbulence below an object will cause a reduction in upward pressure (upthrust) and the object will move into this lower pressure area, i.e. float lower in the water, or even sink, until the turbulence is removed.

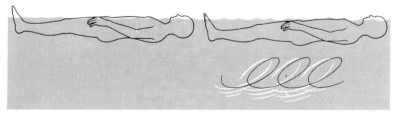

Fig. 49 Creating turbulence below a swimmer (right) will cause a reduction in upthrust and the body will float lower in the water

By creating turbulence beneath objects with a relative density close to 1.0 (e.g. coffee jar lids or lightweight plastic balls with holes in them), the effect of decreasing upthrust can be seen clearly.

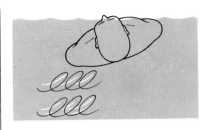

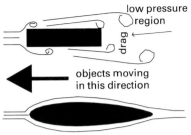

Fig. 50 Turbulence created to one side of a swimmer will decrease the upthrust on that side, causing a roll

Fig. 51 The smooth flow of water around a short wide object (top) breaks up, causing turbulence. A streamlined object such as a fish (bottom), rounded at the front and tapered behind, creates little turbulence

Similarly, turbulence beneath a floating swimmer will cause him to sink lower in the water. Turbulence created to one side of the swimmer will decrease the upthrust on that side, causing a roll.

Although a swimmer just learning to float needs to have water as still as possible, a swimmer with a severe tendency to roll, say to the right, can be helped by creating a little turbulence under his left shoulder (or vice versa). For the more competent swimmer, creating turbulence round them can be a challenge.

Movement through water

Turbulence can cause propulsion. In creating areas of low pressure by movements of the body, the swimmer can move through the water. Adequate changes in pressure can be caused by even small movements, useful for swimmers with limited movements or muscle power.

'Impedance' to movement

While turbulence can create movement, it can also impede it. The smooth flow of water around a short wide object breaks up, leaving behind it an area of swirling water, resulting in unwanted turbulence. The faster the forward movement, the greater this effect. A streamlined object such as a fish, rounded at the front and tapered behind, creates little adverse turbulence. To maximise forward movement, all of the swimmer's energy should be used to create low pressure areas in front of rather than behind the body.

10

Teaching in the water

No matter how experienced an instructor may be, there is always more to learn about teaching swimming. True, the Halliwick Method lays down a carefully designed programme for teaching swimming effectively. It provides instructions with clearly identified and progressive targets to aim for at all ability levels. Within the programme structure, though, instructors are able and indeed encouraged to develop their own personal style of teaching.

Usually in the Halliwick system there are two different teaching roles – 'instructors' are each responsible for a particular swimmer, while the 'group leaders' direct the group sessions. In well established clubs there may also be a chief instructor who is responsible for the whole session. This way of organising sessions not only helps to direct each swimmer's learning in the most effective way, it also provides a structure for training the instructors.

Role of instructors

Individual instructors are the linchpins of the Halliwick system. They don't need to have taught before; often, completely inexperienced people find it quite easy to work with a particular swimmer. This is the strength of the group teaching situation. Under the guidance of a skilled tutor, and with time and experience, an instructor can develop from an enthusiastic beginner into a highly competent teacher.

At first an instructor may feel overwhelmed by how little he knows, but he should not become discouraged. The most important attributes are a genuine desire to help and a firm belief in the value of activity in water.

Instructors must always be aware of the group leader's intentions. In a busy or noisy pool it is particularly important to be good 'listeners' and 'watchers'.

Swimmers usually appreciate the individual attention they receive from their instructors. If an instructor's personal communication skills are good, this will help motivate the swimmer: this, in turn, influences progress. Instructors need, then, to develop a good relationship with their swimmers and become very sensitive to their individual needs. Establishing eye contact is always important, not least when working with swimmers who are either hyperactive or withdrawn.

Supporting and handling techniques should be technically correct and should be used with confidence. They must be appropriate both to the particular water activities and to the needs of the swimmer.

Role of group leaders

The group leader plans and directs the session for a particular ability group. A successful leader knows how to teach swimming, is well prepared for the lesson, and has good communication and observation skills.

Knowledge

As you train, teach and read about swimming therapy, you will gradually improve your teaching. You will need to learn how to break skills down into small, achievable stages for the swimmers, and to be able to reinforce this learning with suitable games and activities. Knowing how to advise instructors and how to correct their supporting techniques is also an important part of a group leader's role.

Preparation

Confident teaching comes much more easily if you are well prepared, so plan thoroughly. First, identify the most important skill for the group to work towards, then plan out a number of appropriate activities for them to practise.

Think through in advance the organisation of each session so that you have all the right equipment ready and you use the available water space sensibly. It helps to write down what you intend doing beforehand, and afterwards to review what worked well or what needs re-thinking.

If you have plenty of ideas you will be able to take a flexible approach to the session, but there should always be a logical sequence to the way in which various activities follow one another.

Sessions should be progressive, varied and stimulating, and group activities (including singing, games and competitions) will help make them so.

Communication

A good group leader will be able to hold the group's interest and attention throughout the session and will know how to make the swimmer or instructor understand what he wants them to do. A friendly and encouraging attitude will always help to create good relationships. Use short, simple speech, backed up by clear visual demonstrations if you feel this is needed. The actual teaching position will vary according to the activity you are doing. Teaching in water is the most effective way of communicating with your group.

Observation

As a group leader becomes more experienced, he will learn how to observe and assess the performance of both swimmers and instructors. Regular practice will teach him the skills of being aware of the whole group while watching each individual carefully, and responding to what he sees. Activities may need to be altered or adapted frequently to suit individuals, without changing the theme of the session.

Creating a good learning environment

The learning process of people with special needs is far more important than merely acquiring the ability to swim. The aim of swimming therapy is to place people into a stimulating environment where personal and social development can take place alongside physical skills. Everyone involved has a part to play in creating a supportive, social, happy atmosphere where individuals can respond successfully to new challenges.

11

Games/activities and group work

Reasons for using games and activities

Many of the basic skills taught by the AST can be incorporated in games and water activities, either for practising a new skill or for recapping one already learnt.

It is natural for children to learn through play. Using the water as a playground, both children and adults find that games are an enjoyable way of gaining confidence and mastering the principles of water safety. Learning through games is a pleasurable way to understand movement, balance and stability, how to change the shape and position of the body, and correct breathing control.

Those who live with a disability often miss out on active participation in group games. However, in the pool – with no restrictive aids – there can be much greater involvement and integration.

The syllabus for the AST proficiency tests and badges lays the foundation on which to base these activities, aligned as it is to the teaching programme of the Halliwick Method. It also provides guidelines for the order in which the swimmer will usually be ready to accept the activities.

35   *All by myself*

70

Advantages of group work

Some of the advantages of learning in a group are:

- new instructors can be involved and learn while helping
- swimmers with difficulties in understanding can copy others
- swimmers who excel help others to try harder
- those lacking in confidence will often try because everyone else is achieving
- there is usually less tension when surrounded by others trying for a similar objective, than for a swimmer working individually
- water space is used more economically.

Groups are made up by:

- similar ability in the water, **not** by reason of disability on land
- age and height of swimmers, which determines required water depth (programmes should suit children, teenagers or adults)
- pace of working – some swimmers need a slower programme and more time to make a movement.

The size of a group is determined by:

- the area of pool available
- the ability of the group leader to control the group
- the skills being taught
- the number of swimmers with similar water ability.

A very workable group would be five swimmers with their instructors.

The group leader runs the programme; the instructors are inter-preters, the link between the leader and their particular swimmers, giving just the right amount of help required at each stage, working towards disengagement.

Remember the maxim: *Help is only help if it is needed!* Often one hears: 'But there are not all that many instructors – there is only me'. One possible solution is to enlist the help of a nearby school, with the older students undertaking a community project and helping as instructors.

Formation for games and activities

With a reminder that we work one-to-one with an instructor as long as help is needed, the following symbols will be used:

S – swimmer
I – instructor

Varying the game formations will create greater interest. The following are easily adaptable when planning programmes.

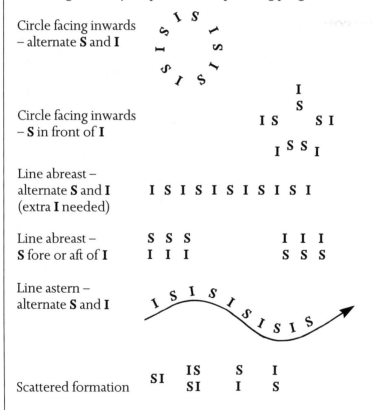

Circle facing inwards
– alternate **S** and **I**

Circle facing inwards
– **S** in front of **I**

Line abreast –
alternate **S** and **I**
(extra **I** needed)

Line abreast –
S fore or aft of **I**

Line astern –
alternate **S** and **I**

Scattered formation

Snake

A very useful way of getting a scattered group together in the pool is with a 'snake'. The leader collects the instructors and their swimmers by calling them to 'Join on the snake!' in line astern. With swimmers in front of instructors (who can give any needed support), it is great fun to 'Catch the tail'. As the 'head' moves around, the 'body' of the snake leans outwards, thus making it simple to catch the 'tail'. When caught, the 'tail' of instructor and swimmer is pulled off and becomes the new 'head', so everyone gets a turn. At the finish of the game, the group is in a circle formation for the next activity.

Game construction

The construction of a game is built around the skill to be highlighted and developed – basic movements, balance, change of shape, breathing, head control, the use of turbulence and upthrust, treading water, floating, propulsion and water safety.

Even though the activities are in the form of 'games', the position of swimmers and instructors, the breathing, the movement of heads and limbs, must be correct. An incorrect pattern, adopted by a swimmer in the early stages of learning, will be very difficult to change later. The activities must be adaptable to the swimmer's level of progress. No two groups are alike, so build or adapt games that help specific swimmers to progress. Often, more than one teaching point can be incorporated.

Explain the activity briefly and clearly so that both swimmers and instructors understand. If equipment is being used (e.g. quoits, plastic eggs or balls), have it to hand.

If the game is successful and popular, use it again and extend it. If it gets a 'thumbs down' from the participants, scrap it and think again.

Singing and the use of music help considerably to set the required pace and encourage the swimmers to relax.

An activity can be used in three forms:

- with the swimmer unaware of the teaching point of the game
- with the swimmer aware of the teaching point, and being assisted
- with the swimmer aware of the teaching point, but not assisted

Many activities lead to winning and losing – such is life. But often it is better to praise the 'triers' and the 'achievers' rather than the winners – the best rather than the first home.

35a   *Waiting in the wheelchair*   35b   *Action in the water*

Always encourage the swimmers to do a little more than they think they can do. They will frequently surprise both themselves and the instructors.

In planning a game, consider the skills required, the ability of the group, and the activity's appeal. Planning your programme over several weeks is a wonderful help, and making a personal reference chart of games in relation to stages of learning is also very useful (*see* chart on page 88).

Bear in mind the age of swimmers when choosing games: children like repetition and story games; teenagers prefer a hint of adventure and challenge; adults relish involvement in working through the skills; senior citizens enjoy those games that they were left out of as children because of disability, and will delight in catching up. Everyone can become much 'younger' in the element of water. Grandparents often say they welcome the games so that they can play with their grandchildren.

There follows some of the activities which have proved popular and helpful in producing a safe and happy swimmer. Each is named for easy identification. (For correct supports, *see* chapter 4.)

Games and activities

Adjustment to water and disengagement

Humpty Dumpty

Age group   – children.

36 Humpty Dumpty had a great fall!

Formation	– line abreast, **S** sitting on poolside, facing **I** in the pool.
Description	– entry to **I** on the word 'Fall', then movement is continued by jumping around pool to remainder of rhyme.
Teaching point	– correct entries from aided to unaided.
Check	– head and hands forwards, and blowing.
Variation	– for teenagers, substitute scuba diving, etc.

Blow bubble catch

Age group	– all ages.
Formation	– circle facing inwards, alternate **I** & **S**.
Description	– one **I** (with or without **S**) in centre, dodging around to tap the head of anyone (**I** & **S**) not blowing bubbles.
Teaching point	– when the face is near the water, 'Blow!'.
Check	– **S** is happy with water near face.
Variation	– underwater catch, with head submerged.

Flip the egg

Age group	– all ages.
Formation	– line abreast, **I** behind **S**. Support as appropriate.
Description	– plastic eggs to be flipped over and over across pool, using 'blow' only – no hands.
Teaching point –	rhythmic blowing, in preparation for swimming.
Check	– **S** position. Hands forwards, shoulders in the water.
Variation	– count flip-overs: ask for at least 5, then for every blow to be a flip.

Water bicycles

Age group	– children.
Formation	– line abreast, **I** behind **S**.
Description	– **I**'s arms inside **S**'s arms – flat handlebars.
Teaching point –	head control; also balance and breathing.
Check	– there must be a gap between **I** & **S** for head control to be achieved.
Variation	– (a) exercise bikes – no forward movement until position is right
	(b) racing bikes – competition across pool
	(c) scattered group – with **S** 'steering': head control
	(d) uphill and downhill – for blowing into the water
	(e) unicycles – support at centre of balance.

1.0m.

37   Flip the egg

38   Kangaroo jumps

Kangaroo jumps

Age group	– all ages.
Formation	– line abreast or scattered.
Description	– **S** facing **I**, who will travel backwards. Support as appropriate.
Teaching point	– feel of upthrust and buoyancy of water; also breathing control and balance.
Check	– these are not 'jumps', but 'bounces', using buoyancy, not gravity. So lift and lower both feet together by bringing the knees up and down. The shoulders are at water level throughout. Note: **I**s walk, not bounce.
Variation	– (a) **I** gives one-hand support, then no support, but hands near
	(b) **S**s bounce backwards, with **I**s behind, giving hip support if necessary
	(c) change to jumping for balance control, making the jumps high, long or to the side.

Water has weight

Age group	– all ages.
Formation	– circle alternate **S** & **I**. Side support as appropriate.
Description	– circle revolves clockwise, leaning and pushing

39 *Water has weight*

sideways until the water is swirling quite fast (3-4 revolutions). On the call 'Change', all push the water anti-clockwise. Repeat.

Teaching point – water is turbulent and heavy, and has to be pushed.

Check – **I** & **S** walk sideways without crossing the feet or turning the shoulders.

Variation – water wheel: same formation but **S** in long-float position. **I**s push the circle around and change direction.

Seaweed or swinging

Age group – all ages.

Formation – individual pairs, scattered. **S** in back-float position. Support from behind at centre of balance.

Description – **S** (completely passive) is swung slowly in a wide arc from side to side.

Teaching point – feel of water and relaxation.

Check – movement is rhythmic, not forced. **I** is stably balanced, and walking backwards very slowly.

Variation – 'Round the rocks': **I** moves backwards, swinging **S** in a wide arc, with a tipping action outwards, letting **S** control the roll.

Further games

Follow-my-leader	– actions geared to the ability of the group.
London Bridge	– singing, with the group line astern going under an arch (formed by a **S** & **I**) which gets lower and lower each time round.
How few steps	– get across the pool. Lift a leg as high as possible and lean forwards on it for a huge stride.

Teaching vertical rotations

Eggs for breakfast

Age group	– children/all ages.
Formation	– circle facing inwards, **S** in front of **I**.
Description	– 'supper-time' – **S** in chair position; 'bed-time' – **S** heads back to float. Leader announces breakfast at 8am and begins to count 5am, 6am, 7am. On the call '8am', plastic eggs are dropped into the circle, and **S** makes a forward recovery to grab an egg with both hands coming forwards.
Teaching point	– rotation from 'chair' to 'bed' to 'chair', and so on.
Check	– **S** is not pushed forwards by over-enthusiastic **I**. Also, **S** changes shape using head, shoulders and hands.
Variation	– use less eggs than the number of **S**s.

40 *Eggs for breakfast*

Catch a foot

Age group	– all ages.
Formation	– circle as 'Eggs for breakfast'.
Description	– similar to 'Eggs for breakfast'. **S** starts in chair position, then head back to float, all feet meeting in the centre. On the call of 'Catch a foot', a forward rotation to chairs, attempting to catch the foot of another **S**.
Teaching point	– head back to float is a slower movement; head forwards to stand is a faster movement. Encourage **S**s to get hands forwards to catch a foot, and to get their own feet down to prevent capture.
Check	– **S** remembers to blow.
Variation	– 'Ball and stick': circle alternate **S** & **I**. Change of shape from round ball (tucked) to long stick (long float) and repeat.

Rag dolls

Age group	– all ages.
Formation	– line abreast, alternate **I** & **S**, plus one extra **I** as side support when appropriate.
Description	– **I** walks backwards, **S** in a relaxed back float. **I** changes direction to walking forwards, and **S**, using head movement only, makes a vertical rotation to prone floating position.
Teaching point	– importance of head control for vertical rotation, and breathing control in prone position.
Check	– depth of water will determine whether rotation is full-length or tucked. Swimmer's ability to control breathing, turning head to the side for breath in.

Sun, wind and rain

Age group	– all ages.
Formation	– circle alternate **I** & **S**. Support as appropriate.
Description	– on the call 'The sun is shining', all **S**s lie back to sunbathe. On the call 'The wind is blowing', all **S**s rotate body to blow to centre of circle. Repeat. To end game, all sunbathers are told 'April

41   Sun, wind and rain

showers' and feet create splash in centre.

Teaching point – head control, vertical rotation and blowing.

Check   – water depth.

Variation   – (a) spare **I** or **S** in centre who enjoys sun, shivers in the wind, and gets very wet in the shower!

– (b) 'Simon says: Feet in! Feet out!'
Formation, teaching point and support as above. Description – 'Feet in' to centre – **S**s in back float. 'Feet out' of circle – **S**s in prone float. But the call is only heeded if 'Simon says', otherwise **S**s remain as they are. Check – depth of water for full-length or tucked rotation.

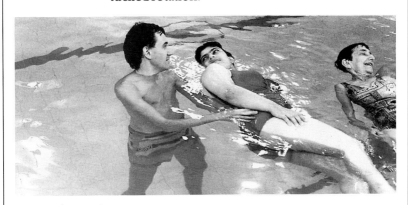

42   Look at me!

Lateral rotation control – rolling

Look at me!

Age group	– all ages.
Formation	– individual pair (**I** & **S**) or scattered group.
Description	– **S** is in back float position. **I**'s head is beside **S**'s left ear, and support is at **S**'s centre of balance. **I** quarter-rotates **S** to the right, then says 'Look at me!'. **S** turns head strongly to **I**. Further rolling is restricted and **S** will regain balance. Repeat on other side with **I**'s head by **S**'s right ear, and quarter-rotate to the left.
Teaching point	– control of lateral balance by using the head.
Check	– let **S** feel the rotation, checking it with the head.
Variation	– 'Round the rocks': *see variation* in 'Seaweed or swinging'.

Pass the ring

Age group	– all ages.
Formation	– line abreast, **S** in front of **I**, in back float position.
Description	– **S** at left end of line has quoit or other easily handled object in left hand. **S** passes object low across body to left hand of next **S**, then regains balance, using head. When object reaches end of line, **S** transfers it to right hand and it is passed back using right hands.
Teaching point	– use of head in controlling lateral rolling.
Check	– ring goes from left hand to left hand, or right hand to right hand. No changing hands while it is

43   Pass the ring

travelling down the line.

Variation – (a) 'Roll to the bar' – extending the same movement to a recovery to the bar at the poolside after a back swim

(b) 'Roll to the gap' – circle formation, one spare **I**. **S** on the right makes a complete lateral roll to the spare **I**. Next **S** then rolls to the gap left by that **S**, and so on until all **S**s are back in original places.

Combined rotations

Fishes in the net

Age group – all ages.

Formation – circle, alternate **S** & **I**. Long-arm support.

Description – **S**s take turns at being 'fish' in the circular net. Escape from the net is under the arms of the circle, re-entry is over the arms, with a combined rotation.

43a   Fishes in the net

Teaching point	– the need to use more than one rotation in certain situations.
Check	– if several fish are re-entering net, take turns, one at a time, to avoid head collision. Fish should not escape over the arms as this could lead to accidents such as hitting the pool wall.
Variation	– play the game with the circle moving.

Upthrust and buoyancy

Hear your number

Age group	– all ages.
Formation	– circle, alternate **I** & **S**, with hand support.
Description	– **I**s count slowly 1, 2, 3, 4, etc. On '1', **S**s submerge, breathing out slowly. Their number is that which they hear on surfacing. The highest number is the winner.
Teaching point	– difficulty of staying under water. Reassurance that water pushes us up. Breathing: 'Never hold your breath'.
Check	– blowing and humming. Position of body.
Variation	– (a) no **I** contact while submerged (b) picking up an object from the pool floor.

King of the sea

Age group	– children.
Formation	– circle. Long- or short-arm support, with ability.
Description	– group leader explains: 'King Neptune, who lives at the bottom of the sea, has invited you all to tea. He always serves fizzy lemonade, so we want to see bubbles'. Chant **S** says: 'We're going to tea with the king of the sea.' **I** replies: 'And when are you coming back?' On 'back', **S**s submerge and **I**s chant 'Monday, Tuesday, Wednesday, etc'. Note Some swimmers manage a week or more.
Teaching point	– upthrust of water and breathing control.
Check	– position of body. No breath holding.
Variation	– extend to no **I** contact, then to bringing back 'cakes' (coffee jar lids) from pool floor.

44   King of the
sea

Further games

Find the frog/quoit/plate, etc on the floor of pool.

Pirates' treasure	– coffee jar lids, with a value painted on each, e.g. 3, 5, 10. **S**s collect hoard (one lid at a time). Extend to collecting a set value, e.g. 40. Eyes must be open to select value.

Balance at rest

Stars and mushrooms

Age group	– all ages.
Formation	– scattered (**S**s independent).
Description	– if in shallow water, start in chair position; if in deep water, start by treading water. Group leader calls a shape, e.g. 'Stars', and counts down '5, 4, 3, 2, 1', giving **S**s time to balance motionless in the shape called. Return to start position. Repeat with other shapes.
Teaching point	– balance at rest, relaxed stillness.
Check	– position of head, breathing.

45   Stars and
mushrooms

46   Sink the ship

Variation	– many other shapes may be called. Call shapes which water will not balance without causing a rotation, e.g. mushroom float on back, face upwards.

Sink the ship

Age group	– all ages.
Formation	– circle, alternate **S** & **I**, facing inwards.
Description	– one **S** takes up a balanced float in the centre. Then the circle moves clockwise, as in 'Water has weight', causing turbulence in which the 'ship' must balance to a count of ten. **S**s take turns at being the 'ship'.
Teaching point	– balance at rest while water is moving. Feeling and using all rotational patterns. **S**s finish with a forward recovery in the centre.
Check	– limit the turbulence created to the **S**s ability to cope. **I**s may assist **S**s to balance at first, if necessary.
Variation	– change the circle movement to jumping ten times while moving around, creating greater turbulence.

Maintaining balance while moving

Space ships

Age group	– all ages.
Formation	– scattered in pairs (**I** & **S**).
Description	– **I** (space capsule) envelops **S** (astronaut) within

47   *Space ships*

circled arms and locked hands. **S** presses ear of
I to unlock door of capsule. Then, using hands
only (no leg movement), **S** moves out of doorway,
circles capsule, enters door again and presses other
ear to lock it.

Teaching point – head controls balance. Disengagement.

Check – keep hands together and chin near hands for
balance. No leg movement.

Variation – whole group links into a large space station, and
two 'astronauts' have to open the door and circuit
the station (either travelling in the same or
opposite directions).

Round the yard-arm

Age group – all ages.

Formation – singly with **I**. Water deeper than **S**'s height.

Description – **I** has right hand on the rail and right foot on the
wall, both sideways to the pool wall, left arm and
leg extended out. Starting at the rail and using
hand-holds only, **S** moves along **I**'s right arm,
across **I**'s front, out along the left arm, round **I**'s
hand, returning along the back of **I** to the rail.

Teaching point – head control. Disengagement.

Check – **S** is safe in deep water before attempting this.

It is a good idea to compile a list for quick and easy reference to
identify the teaching point required. Here is an example to help you:

48 Round the yard-arm. This is harder than you think. Try it.

Teaching point	Activity/game
Adjustment to water and disengagement	Humpty Dumpty, Blow bubble catch, Kangaroo jumps, Water has weight, Water bicycles, Follow-my-leader, Canoes & motor boats, London Bridge, Mulberry bush, How few steps, Snake
Vertical rotation	Eggs for breakfast, Sun, wind and rain, Rag dolls, Catch a foot, Simon says, Ball and stick
Lateral rotation	Look at me!, Round the rocks, Pass the ring, Roll to the gap
Combined rotations	Fishes in the net, Falling in, Falling over
Using upthrust	Pirates' treasure, King of the sea, Hear your number
Balance (at rest)	Stars and mushrooms
Balance (moving)	Space ships, Sink the ship, Round the yard-arm
Using turbulence	Come with me
Simple progression and basic movement	Rowing boats, How few strokes, Gliding, Motor boats

12

Progress of a swimmer

The structure of the Halliwick Method can provide many indications of the progress of a swimmer, the most obvious being water skills. There are, however, other benefits – improved movement on the land, enhancement of the ability to dress and undress, and personal hygiene – all of which encourage independent living. Communication can become more effective. Speech is encouraged; but if that is not possible, other sounds and signs such as mime are used by the instructors as well as the swimmers. Water activities can give the individual a chance to make a choice. Above all, courage and initiative develop with water skills and for some it may provide a chance of saving another person's life.

Many instructors have had to learn breathing, balance and relaxation before becoming safe swimmers and good instructors in the water. People with disabilities who have mastered the Halliwick Method can make ideal instructors.

Badge tests

The AST has four proficiency tests to monitor a swimmer's progress towards independence and provide recognition of achievement. These tests are linked to a series of colour coded badges, and cover the skills necessary to achieve water safety. There is also the opportunity to recognise specific achievement with interim certificates or awards. It is necessary for instructors to be able to perform all the skills which they teach in the four badge tests.

AST Proficiency Tests

(Revised 1988, 1990)

Examiners
Red and Yellow Badges: assessed by registered lecturers, holders of the Halliwick Instructor's Certificate, and senior and experienced

instructors. Green and Blue Badges: assessed by registered lecturers, holders of the Halliwick Instructor's Certificate, and external examiners by application to the AST Education Committee. The assessor for Green and Blue Badges must not be a member of the candidate's club, but it is recommended that the senior instructor of the candidate's club should be present during the test.

AST Proficiency Test 1 (Red Badge)

1 Enter the water unaided from a sitting position to an instructor.
2 Blow a plastic 'egg' (with support from behind if necessary) for a distance of 10m (30ft).
3 Perform 'kangaroo jumps' for a distance of 10m (30ft).
4 Perform a forward recovery with a minimum of aid.

AST Proficiency Test 2 (Yellow Badge)

1 Enter the water from the poolside to a stable position in the water, unassisted in any way.
2 Sit on the bottom of the pool, or satisfactorily submerge, and demonstrate ability to breathe out under water.
3 'Kangaroo jump' or walk unaided for a distance of 10m (30ft).
4 Demonstrate a horizontal roll in either direction, with the minimum of aid.
5 Pick up a plate, or like object, from at least 1m (3ft) of water.
6 Demonstrate a mushroom float for a minimum of three seconds.

AST Proficiency Test 3 (Green Badge)

1 Demonstrate ability to enter water from a sitting position unaided.
2 Perform unaided: (a) forward recovery
 (b) rolling recovery.
3 Float motionless for ten seconds or mushroom float for three seconds.
4 Tread water for 60 seconds.
5 Perform a mushroom float with a push down by an instructor to a minimum depth of 1.2m (4ft), followed by an unassisted controlled return to the surface, and then recovery, to a safe breathing position, by use of a lateral rotation.
6 Swim 10m (30ft) by any method.

7 Against a swirl of water, *either* get out over the poolside unaided or, if this is physically impossible, maintain a safe position from which assistance can be given.

AST Proficiency Test 4 (Blue Badge)

For holders of the AST Green Badge only.

Part I To be certified by the Club Chief Instructor before the day of the main test.
1 Swim a distance of 400m (440yds), by any method, without stopping or touching the sides, on a continuous circuit.

Part II To be examined by a recognised external examiner from another club.
1 Swim, on the back, a figure of eight, within an area of 10 x 5m (30 x 15ft).
2 Submerge and push off from the side of the pool, and glide under water to reach the surface without any swimming stroke.
3 Submerge and recover two items, 1m (3ft) apart, from a depth of at least 1m (3ft), without re-surfacing until completion of the collection.
4 Submerge vertically feet first, until the water is 0.5m (1.5ft) above the swimmer's head. Rise to the surface and maintain a vertical position, without touching the bottom, for two minutes or more.

Part III To be examined on the same day and by the same examiner as Part II. These tests to take place in deep water. There is a series of options to enable swimmers without the use of legs and/or arms, or with other specific problems, to perform one skill within each of the disciplines without making a special allowance for their disability. Whenever possible, more than one of each of these skills should be learned, and the swimmer's techniques should be extended and improved.
1 Enter the water head first by:
(a) seal dive using arms only, or
(b) standing dive, or
(c) sitting dive.
2 Perform one of the following:
(a) rotary crawl using arms only

(b) twin tail using legs only
(c) rolling log.
3 Perform one of the following:
(a) washing tub using arms
(b) spinning top using legs
(c) water wheel.
4 Perform one of the following:
(a) back somersault
(b) front somersault
(c) pendulum, completing 1½ swings.

While each badge test emphasises different water skills it is essential, when making an assessment, to check that previous skills have been retained. The swimmer should be capable of performing each activity without the need for reminders or instruction. Each skill should be performed competently, in a relaxed and confident manner, the swimmer demonstrating good breath control and balance, and having his eyes open at all times.

After passing the Green Badge, the swimmer should be safe to enjoy the complete freedom of the pool without the need for an instructor, and with only the watchful eye of a lifeguard to ensure his safety. He should have the confidence to cope with any situation in the club or at a gala.

The Blue Badge is aimed at providing a wide range of water skills which can be tried, practised and perfected over a long period as an alternative to timed swimming for races or distance swimming, both of which can become very boring if this is the staple of club sessions.

Detailed guidelines on the testing of the badges can be obtained from the AST.

Competitive and distance swimming

Within the AST most clubs organise their own galas or 'splash events', which serve as an introduction to competitive swimming. Races are usually swum on a time handicap basis, so that swimmers with all types of disabilities can take part with a chance of winning. This prevents the situation where elite competitors entirely dominate proceedings. Handicapping also broadens the scope of competition available to members.

The natural progression is from club gala to inter-club gala, then to regional gala and eventually to a national gala which is held annually and hosted in turn by the different regions (or ASTRAs – Association of Swimming Therapy Regional Associations) around the country. Help in planning and organising a gala is available from the AST.

Within each club it is usual to award Distance Certificates for the completion of standard distances without the use of swimming aids, and it is also possible for club members to participate in the British Long Distance Swimming Association's annual 'One hour swim'.

In many areas a league competition is held each year to encourage swimmers to meet and mix with others who have similar difficulties and who may perhaps feel that they are not ready to compete in a full scale gala. Open water swims are organised in some areas, offering a different challenge for more competent swimmers. Where experienced swimmers have the opportunity to join local competitive clubs, this should be encouraged.

Records and progress

The progress of all swimmers should be recorded regularly and reviewed at the instructors' meetings, when discussion about special needs and problems can be aired.

It is advisable to re-test swimmers after a long absence, illness, operation or similar lay-off, because they may find that their sense of balance and ability to float has changed, and that they need to relearn some basic skills. As a safety precaution it is always advisable for swimmers transferring from one club to another to have their ability in the water checked. This could take the form of a re-assessment of the badge tests.

Many clubs award progress trophies. These should not be an annual ritual given for the sake of the presentation, but should be awarded to the swimmer (or swimmers) who has made outstanding progress within the limits of his own ability. Recipients should be selected by the instructors after discussion with the chief instructor and group leaders at their regular meetings.

When swimmers who at first sight appear to be severely disadvantaged, reach the standard of achievement which the Halliwick Method produces, they can be justly proud of their attainments.

13

People with disabilities

This chapter is not meant to be seen as a medical student's manual. However, a basic understanding of the more common disabilities should help to generate a greater appreciation of the difficulties facing people with disabilities, and, more importantly, should help to minimise potential problems.

Medical certificate

In addition to the medical certificate that must be produced before joining an AST club, it is helpful if the swimmer's doctor includes details of 'hidden' conditions (fits, diabetes, heart trouble, etc). This information will help instructors and lifeguards to monitor the swimmer's activities. Children taking part in school sessions must have their parents' permission.

Anatomy

Only a limited knowledge of anatomy is assumed: indeed, a detailed knowledge is not required.

It is important to know that the body has a bony framework. Bones are connected together by joints which are controlled by muscles and held together by ligaments. In normal conditions, the muscles are toned or partially prepared for movement. Each muscle is made up of many small muscle fibres which are supplied with blood from the heart via the blood vessels (arteries, capillaries and veins).

Nerves from the brain transmit nerve impulses (small electric discharges) to the muscles. Paralysis of the muscles may result if the nerves or brain are damaged. This may take one of two forms: a floppy (flaccid) or a tense (stiff) state, depending on where the damage has occurred.

Ability, not disability

Our philosophy is to stress *ability*, not disability. It is more important to know how the swimmer's physical shape will balance in the water than to have a precise knowledge of his medical condition.

In the water, the swimmer is naturally supported by buoyancy, and so can learn to enjoy freedom from the artificial aids he may need on land. The use of flotation aids (inflated rings, floats, etc) is discouraged because they prolong the period of dependence and create further balance problems when removed.

Water only reacts to two factors – density and shape. Physical disabilities can thus be divided into two categories: those where the body's *density* has a dominant effect, and those where its *shape* has.

Natural floaters

This group comprises swimmers (disabled or not) whose density is relatively less than water. For example:

- the overweight
- those who have wasted, floppy limbs (e.g. caused by muscular dystrophy and spina bifida)
- those with paralysed limbs following a fracture of the spine
- small compact swimmers with short arms and legs (dwarfs).

The great anxiety of natural floaters is not that of sinking, but that of regaining an upright position from a back float position.

Poor floaters

These often include:

- adults with cerebral palsy (either the stiff or wriggly types) – sudden uncontrolled movement of limbs or tensing of muscles
- those with multiple sclerosis
- adults brain damaged following injury, stroke or tumour
- tall, solid, bony or well-muscled people.

Natural rollers

This group includes any condition which makes the body uneven in shape, thus producing an unnatural density distribution:

- amputees
- those born with absent limbs
- hemiplegics, who have one side of their body affected
- those with scoliosis.

General problems

In addition to any obvious handicap, these may include the following:

- acute fear of falling
- difficulty in making themselves understood
- lack of understanding of the spoken word
- lopsided (asymmetric) body
- difficulty in making movements
- inability to control movements
- poor circulation and breathing capacity
- easily damaged skin, bones and joints
- incontinence (lack of control of urine flow and bowel function).

The first visit to the swimming pool is often an emotional time. There may be anxiety, excitement or aggression, so you must expect laughter or tears, or both.

Common disabilities

It is very important for the helpers and instructors to understand the disabilities of their swimmers so that they can be aware of special needs and offer adequate support, emotional as well as physical. The most common disabilities, and suggestions on how to obtain the best and safest results for swimmers with these particular problems, are given here.

Disabilities are found in two forms:

- congenital – problems have been present from birth
- acquired – problems may have been caused by accident, disease or old age.

Absent limbs

Although limbs may be congenitally absent from natural causes, certain drugs taken during the mother's pregnancy are known to in-duce this defect. In the early 1960s a number of children were born without, or with only rudimentary limbs following the use of the drug Thalidimide. Their limitations are physical ones of the limbs, and particular care is needed in diving where there are no arms to protect the head on entry into the water.

Achondroplasia or 'dwarfism'

These swimmers have large heads (but not 'water on the brain') and short arms and legs. They may also have impaired hearing.

Amputees

Amputation may be of arms or legs, partial or complete. The majority of amputations are to the lower limbs. Special care on the poolside is required, so use ambulance chairs or canvas lifting seats, and keep artificial limbs dry and near the poolside. Ensure the skin is dry before re-fitting the limb. The poolside is very dangerous for people using walking aids – rubber ferrules on sticks may slip on the wet surface.

Amputees, once balanced in the water, can become very strong swimmers. If the amputation is the result of an operation for a diabetic or circulatory problem, extra care must be taken of the skin, particularly that of the stump.

Arthritis

- *Osteoarthritis* involves swelling, stiffness and pain in weight-bearing joints. It can be caused by an accident or ageing.
- *Rheumatoid arthritis* is a generalised inflammatory condition affecting many joints, usually starting in the hands and feet, and often associated with poor general health. Water activities causing discom-fort should be discontinued.

Asthma

Allergy plays a large part in this condition, and the consequent diffi-culty in breathing can cause problems. Swimming is a particularly suitable sport for this disability group with its emphasis on breathing control and exposure to a moist atmosphere. Make sure that asth-matics do not become over-tired or stand around getting cold.

Autism

This condition is a life-long developmental disorder characterised by difficulties in forming and maintaining social relationships, problems with language and non-verbal communication, and resistance to change.

It is important that you take the time to ensure that you have the swimmer's attention before giving clear, uncomplicated instructions. This may be difficult because people with autism frequently fail to make appropriate eye contact and may engage in distracting repetitive behaviour.

Initially, there may be a need to work one-to-one in a corner of the pool for some weeks, or even months.

Changes in routine can produce severe adverse reactions, so you may find it useful to conduct a well-structured session with a consistent outline from week to week.

Brain damage

This may result from an injury at birth, an accident, or brain tumour, and can cause physical or mental disability, and possibly give rise to visual or hearing problems. Many people with brain damage have great difficulty in co-ordination and concentration. Clumsy children may fall into this category, displaying the above symptoms in a less severe form.

Cerebral palsy or 'spastic'

This condition also results from damage to the brain, leading to balance and movement problems. It is sometimes accompanied by learning difficulties and epilepsy. There are three main types of cerebral palsy.

- *Athetoid cerebral palsy* is marked by unco-ordinated, involuntary movement, resulting often in writhing, wriggling limbs. It is frequently accompanied by poor head control and considerable difficulties with speech and swallowing. Efforts to control movement cause grimacing and increased motion.
- *Spastic cerebral palsy* is characterised by muscle spasm and jerky

movements, often with rigidity. The swimmer may suffer from paralysis of the body down one side (hemiplegia) or of all four limbs (tetraplegia). The arms are often bent up close to the body and the legs stretched out or crossed in a scissor position. Circulation is poor because of rigidity. Speech can be impaired.

• *Ataxic cerebral palsy* is characterised by a staggering gait and the inability to make rapid co-ordinated movements.

People with cerebral palsy may have poor breath control and difficulty in keeping the mouth closed. Therefore, they can either inhale water and choke, or swallow water involuntarily and vomit. Learning to blow or hum is therefore very important.

They can be excitable but often enjoy and benefit from the relative relaxation of muscle spasm which occurs during swimming sessions. If they are able to swim, they improve control, speed and stroke the longer they are in the water, and they are better in long rather than short races.

Give them time to adjust and do not take away their independence by rushing to their aid. They know when and where they need help.

People with cerebral palsy may have impaired hearing and considerable perceptual problems, and may suffer from fits.

Colostomies

For various medical reasons, people may have surgery to divert the bowel or, more rarely now, the ureter, to the abdominal wall where the waste products are collected in a plastic bag attached to the body by an adhesive plaster. Bags should be emptied before entering the pool to reduce the chance of an accident. If leakage is a problem, extra absorbent tissue should be applied over the bag and plastic pants worn. When coming out over the side of the pool, the swimmer should lift his body high enough to prevent the bag being dragged out of position. If this is not possible, he should be assisted out with a horizontal lift.

Curvature of the spine

• *Scoliosis* is a lateral curvature of the spine.
• *Kyphosis* is a forward curvature of the spine. This gives rise to hump-back deformity.

Cystic fibrosis

This is an hereditary disease which affects the pancreas and gives rise to poor absorption of food. These swimmers suffer with chronic chest infections. They may cough, so have tissues to hand.

Diabetes

In this condition, the pancreas does not function adequately and the body is unable to control the level of blood sugar. Many diabetics are overweight and suffer from arthritic joints, especially hips, knees and ankles. The circulation may be affected and this gives rise to increasing problems with sight, skin infections and ulceration. In serious conditions, amputation of limbs is needed to prevent the spread of gangrene.

Dislocated hips

Children may be born with dislocated hips or may develop a condition known as 'Perthes' disease', an uncommon condition caused by fragmentation of the head of the femur. Both may be treated with splints and during this time the child must not be allowed to take his weight on the affected side. Hip dislocation may be a complication in some people suffering from cerebral palsy.

Epilepsy

The question of whether people with epilepsy should swim has aroused controversy for many years, not least among members of the medical profession. The National Co-ordinating Committee on Swimming for People with Disabilities, in conjunction with the British Epilepsy Association, has produced a special leaflet called 'Swimming and epilepsy'. See page 124 for details.

An epileptic attack is due to an occasional sudden abnormal impulse from the brain cells. Epilepsy itself is an established tendency to recurring fits. Anyone can have a fit if the insult or stress to the brain is great enough. This occurs in people of all ages, social backgrounds and levels of intellect.

There are three main types of attack:

• major seizures (*grand mal*) are convulsive fits. Here, the person holds his breath, the limbs go into spasm, and unconsciousness

occurs. During the attack, convulsive movements occur and afterwards the swimmer may become confused or tired for some time.
• absences (*petit mal*) are single short periods of vagueness with loss of comprehension. Such attacks may be repeated.
• psychomotor fits vary a great deal, but often consist of automatic actions associated with clouding of consciousness. The person appears to be conscious but is unable to respond during the attack.

All swimmers with epilepsy must be watched while they are at the pool, and appropriate action taken if a fit occurs in or out of the water.

First aid for epileptic fits on land

• Keep calm: a fit cannot be stopped once it has started.
• Ease the person to the floor and loosen any tight clothing.
• Prevent him from hurting himself on furniture or the poolside.
• Turn him on his side so that the saliva runs out of the mouth.
• Do not attempt to insert anything between his teeth.
• As the fit subsides the person will be exhausted, so allow him to sleep if he wishes.

First aid for epileptic fits in the water

• After a minor attack, the swimmer should be helped quietly and calmly out of the pool.
• During a major attack, the swimmer's face must be kept above the water until the attack subsides.
• Ideally, the swimmer should be supported in shallow water. If the attack occurs in deep water, the swimmer should be moved to a depth where the life-saver can safely stand.
• Remove the swimmer from the pool when movement has ceased, then continue to handle as on land.
• If expired air resuscitation has been necessary, medical advice should be obtained.

Fragilitis ossium/osteogenesis imperfecta (brittle bones)

People with this condition are small and their limbs are defomed by frequent fractures. Deafness can be an associated disability. Great care should be taken on the side of the pool and when entering or leaving the water.

Haemophilia

This is a congenital condition, affecting mainly males, where a minor injury causes excessive bruising. Bleeding into joints causes pain, swelling and stiffness, and may lead to an arthritic condition. Those with haemophilia should swim only in a controlled environment and care must be taken to ensure that they do not bang or bump their bodies either in the water or on the poolside. Handling must never be rough or too firm.

Hydrocephalus

This is an enlargement of the head due to excess fluid round or within the brain tissue, often associated with spina bifida. Hydrocephalus is relieved by a plastic tube containing a valve (or 'shunt') which draws the fluid from the space in the brain into the blood system. The tube usually lies under the skin on the right side of the neck, so extra care should be taken in handling the head and neck.

Incontinence

An inability to control the bladder and/or bowel results in wetting and/or soiling. This may be associated with neurological conditions such as spinal injury, spina bifida, etc, or with severe learning difficulties.

- Urinary incontinence is commonly managed by the insertion of a catheter to drain the bladder, frequently into a plastic bag. The bag should be emptied every two to four hours. (This is often managed by the swimmer.) If the catheter is controlled by a spigot, then urine should be released every 20 to 30 minutes.
- Faecal incontinence may be controlled by regular toileting routine, assisted by diet.

Learning difficulty

This was previously called 'mental handicap' or 'educational subnormality' and may be classed as 'severe' (SLD) or 'moderate'

(MLD). The problem affects learning, understanding, concentration, short term memory and ability to communicate.

Children with learning difficulties may be hyperactive and emotionally disturbed. Others have spatial problems with a resulting poor body image. They benefit from working with other children. They also require clear and simple explanations and demonstrations: activities need structure and repetition. Discipline is essential.

There are many causes of the problem which may have been present from birth or acquired after an illness, such as meningitis or injury to the brain. Down's syndrome, previously known as 'mongolism', commonly results in learning difficulties.

The facial characteristics are easily recognised. As children they are late in walking, caused by poor muscle tone and lax joints. Co-ordination is poor because of a lack of motor control. There is an inadequate body awareness. People with Down's syndrome may have limited sight and hearing. They may also have a heart lesion and often suffer from chest and ear infections. As children they may have no idea of danger. They are well known extroverts.

Children with severe learning difficulties benefit a great deal from water activities. Water stimulates through the skin (extrinsically) or may stimulate the inner person (intrinsically). Whichever way, or both, swimmers may begin to respond and make some effort to move their limbs.

Close supervision in the changing rooms and on the poolside, as well as in the water, is essential for all people suffering from learning difficulties.

Multiple sclerosis

This is a progressive condition where isolated areas of degeneration occur throughout the nervous system, producing a variety of signs and symptoms. As paralysis increases, the limbs tend to become tight or spastic: there is a loss of sensation and poor blood circulation. Incontinence may occur. Vision and speech can be affected. In some cases, people with this condition seem to have more energy and better control of their limbs when in the water. Often they are euphoric. Assist when required, but help them maintain their independence for as long as possible. They become tired quickly and should not be over-stretched. Times in competition swims are very variable and become progressively slower.

Muscular dystrophy

This progressive disease of the muscles starts in childhood. Considerable psychological support is necessary. The muscles lose their power and are replaced by fibrous tissue. Gradually the paralysed limbs develop deformities of the joints. Owing to inactivity, the young person puts on a great deal of weight. The circulation is poor and skin is easily damaged. Eventually the respiratory muscles are affected and swimming must be discontinued. Great care is needed, as for multiple sclerosis.

Parkinson's disease

A progressive disease of older people, this is also known as 'paralysis agitans' because there is constant movement of the hands and feet. The limbs gradually become spastic, balance is affected, and the loss of sensation and the poor circulation cause problems. Care is similar to that for those with cerebral palsy (see page 98).

Poliomyelitis

This is a viral infection attacking the nerve cells of communication between the spinal cord and muscles, resulting in paralysed (weak or floppy) muscles. This paralysis may be an isolated weakness of a muscle or may be widespread paralysis of a whole limb. If this is so, there may well be deformity of the limb due to muscle wastage and fibrous contractions. Affected limbs have a poor blood supply and skin damage is a considerable hazard. Great care must be taken, as for spina bifida (see page 105).

Polyneuritis

An infection of the spinal cord produces generalised weakness and flail limbs. Poor circulation and sensory loss allow the skin to be easily damaged. Care should be similar to that for spina bifida (see page 105).

Rubella syndrome

This may affect a child whose mother contracted German measles during pregnancy. Such children are under-sized and clumsy in their movements, and have learning difficulties. Co-ordination is not easy and they often suffer from hearing loss. There may also be a congenital heart lesion and/or sight difficulties.

Sensory disabilities

Deafness may be partial or complete. It usually makes balance more difficult. Many deaf people lip-read or use sign language. Since deaf aids cannot be worn in water, communication should be by facial expression and hand signs. Deaf children often compensate by concentrating on visual signals, and they are excellent mimics.

Visual disability, like deafness, can be of varying degrees. Partial sight is quite common in congenital handicaps. Many blind people concentrate on hearing skills, and find their way about by sensing vibrations in the air and water. Those who have a detached retina must avoid knocks and strenuous activities including diving.

Sensory loss

This includes loss of feeling and inability to feel pain, touch, heat and cold, pressure and movement.

- *Anaesthesia* means without feeling.
- *Parathesia* describes tingling ('pins and needles')
- *Hyperthesia* is an excessive sensitivity of the skin. (For care of the skin, refer to the section on spina bifida.)

Skin problems

Burns or skin grafts may cause skin contractures which can restrict movement of joints. Limbs move more freely in water.

Swimmers with skin problems are often very self-conscious and prefer to be covered with towels when waiting on the poolside.

Psoriasis and eczema are chronic non-infectious skin conditions. They may be affected by chemicals used to purify the water, so take special notice of any reaction after swimming. The swimmer should always shower after a swim. Socks are an excellent way to protect feet in danger of abrasion.

Spina bifida

A failure in spinal development before birth results in the spine being divided by a cleft – normally the spinal cord is completely protected by a canal of bone. In this condition the spinal cord is often exposed which leads to varying degrees of paralysis of the lower limbs, and possibly hydrocephalus.

Paralysis of the nerve supply to the bladder and bowel may occur, perhaps causing incontinence.

Meticulous care of the skin is important because of the lack of feeling. The swimmer does not realise that a rough surface will scratch or bruise his limbs or buttocks. Unwary helpers can do real damage which may take months to heal, largely because of the poor blood supply to the skin. A moment of carelessness may cause weeks of unnecessary suffering where the disabled person is unable to wear shoes, callipers or supports, and has to resort to a wheelchair.

In the dressing room or on the poolside, particular attention is needed when handling spina bifida swimmers because the lower limbs are usually very floppy and easily twisted. Great care must be taken so that feet do not trail on the bottom of the pool, or along the ground if the swimmer is in a wheelchair.

Spinal cord paralysis

This is a disease or accident which affects the part of the body supplied by nerves below the level of the injury. The paralysis may be flaccid (floppy) or spastic (stiff, tight) and affects either the lower limbs (paraplegia) or all four limbs (tetraplegia). If the lesion is in the neck, the limbs and muscles of respiration are affected. Below the lesion there is impaired circulation and loss of sensation so that the skin is easily damaged. Sudden precipitation into cold water may lead to an increase in muscle spasms which could cause problems. Otherwise, the difficulties are similar to those of spina bifida – great care is needed with the skin of paralysed limbs.

Stroke

Stroke is caused by an interference to the blood supply to part of the brain and frequently affects only one side of the body, giving rise to the condition of hemiplegia. Speech and vision may also be affected. Remember that limbs that are paralysed for any reason have a poor blood supply. This means that the skin is easily damaged, bones are more easily broken and joints dislocated. Special attention must be taken at all times.

Rehabilitation

Swimming after an injury, operation or heart attack can, under controlled conditions and with medical consent, greatly encourage the body to return to normal functioning. Swimming improves the heart action and the increased circulation restores muscle tone and improves joint movement. Correct handling and an understanding of the swimmer's breathing and balance, which comes with experience, will help the swimmer regain self-confidence and boost his morale.

Elderly people who may never have had the opportunity to swim may get a new lease of life. A more enjoyable social existence is an important bonus of swimming.

A helper or instructor may feel overwhelmed by his lack of knowledge at first, but do not be discouraged. The first and most important requirements are a smile and a genuine enthusiastic wish to help. This attitude will lead to 'self-forgetfulness', which will enable you and your swimmers to feel happy and relaxed. Try to maintain eye contact with your swimmer because this will enable you to discern if he is happy and becoming increasingly confident in the water.

14

Assisting at the pool

The safety of a swimmer is absolutely crucial; if he is hurt at your club, a great deal can be lost. If he is unhappy about the way he is assisted, he may never come again. It is not enough that people with a disability are safe: they must feel safe when being assisted to move on the side *and* in the water. Since assistance on the side comes first, the swimmer's attitude to the session will stem from how he feels before he actually enters the water. Helpers should aim to earn confidence, minimise fuss, and never make people with disabilities feel they are being a nuisance. Laughter and fun are great assets here. Helpers should try to adjust their minds to imagine how people with disabilities feel, recalling what it was like to have a broken leg plastered up from top to bottom, or some such other temporary disablement.

Preparing to help

We all have different levels of ability and most of us need some help at various times. Find out what kind of help is most likely to be needed before the swimming session actually starts. As a helper you may need to do some specific training or you may need to be briefed on the special assistance that some swimmers need. The AST has drawn up guidelines for the teaching of moving and assisting.

Helpers, swimmers, instructors and carers can learn much through talking together and spending a little time with one another to help foster an atmosphere of mutual respect and confidence.

Remember that some disabilities may not be immediately recognisable, so extra care should be taken by both new swimmers and the helpers and instructors.

All club members should be familiar with the layout of the pool and changing rooms, and should identify and note any particular hazards. This is especially important for members with visual problems. While many swimmers are quite capable of moving independently, they may find that the pool demands far more of

49　'Level speaking' with a wheelchair swimmer

them with unusual obstacles such as heavy doors, foot baths and wet floors, and they may need some help in this respect. Keeping the changing area and poolside clear is everyone's responsibility.

During your first few visits as a helper, try to be particularly careful about every small detail. This will help everybody, not only you but also your swimmers, to develop confidence, and everyone will enjoy the swimming session. People with disabilities are entitled to take risks, but the risks must be of their choosing and not as a result of someone else's negligence or misunderstanding.

Changing

We all put a different price on privacy. Some swimmers may be happy to change in a communal changing room where assistance is more accessible, but others may prefer to use a cubicle. Find out what makes your swimmer feel most comfortable both physically and emotionally, and organise where they change accordingly.

There should always be a helper in both male and female changing rooms when swimmers are present.

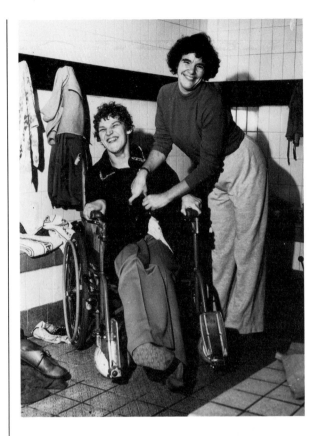

50 Helping
each other

Make it easier

Sensible clothes with a minimum of complicated fastenings, shoes without laces, and velcro in place of buttons, can speed changing considerably.

Ask the swimmers (or carers) how much help is essential, but encourage them increasingly to dress and undress themselves and help each other whenever they can.

Swimmers should feel safe and stable while changing. Some may need to lie down, while others may manage very well from a chair. A bench or table covered with a towel, to avoid slipping and for warmth, may be easier for children.

Clothes should always be placed together, if possible in a bag, to avoid having to search for them when the swimmer comes out of the pool. Valuables should be kept in a safe place.

Dress the upper body first to prevent heat loss. Take particular care not to force stiff limbs and joints into clothes. Where possible follow the swimmer's preferred routine and check that he feels comfortable before he leaves.

Be aware of dangers

As you remove any callipers and braces, see how they work so that you will know what to do to put them on again. Swimmers who rely on braces or appliances for everyday activities may be less stable without them.

Pay special attention to delicate skin, especially areas of the body which have little or no feeling.

Helpers should be aware that jewellery, watches and long nails may scratch; even small injuries may not easily heal, so dress appropriately.

When drying, be very careful because wet skin is susceptible to damage. Try not to be shy about drying the genitals – having to put up with wet underclothes would be a sad way to end a happy swim.

Hygiene

Ideally, everybody should shower both before and after the swim. A shower chair is useful for anybody who has difficulty standing on a wet and slippery floor.

Some swimmers will have particular routines for continence which you need to discuss so that you can make appropriate arrangements. The pool should have facilities for the easy disposal of nappies or pads.

Wheelchair safety

Helpers need to try to familiarise themselves as much as they can with the various types of wheelchairs. Knowing which parts of a chair are removable can be very useful when you are assisting a swimmer and you will know which parts not to hold when folding or lifting the chair.

When a swimmer is moving to and from a wheelchair, always check that the brakes are on. Electric wheelchair users should make certain that their switches are in the 'Off' position before changing or transferring.

See if the footplates can be folded and swung round out of the way to the side of the chair. On some modern wheelchairs, though, they may be fixed, so take extra care.

Some swimmers may like to use their chairs to get to the poolside. Make sure that their feet are placed on the footrests, and do not hit doors or other obstacles. Be wary of injuring other swimmers who may be in your path. Swimmers are particularly vulnerable to injury without their clothing, splints and shoes, and any injuries may take a long time to heal.

Wheelchair users should keep well away from the pool edge and, if possible, park parallel to the pool. The use of graduated stools might be a helpful option for getting up and down from a chair with or without assistance.

Swimmers who usually use an appliance or walking aids, which can be dangerous on wet floors, are advised to use a shower chair or walk with a helper when going to and from the poolside.

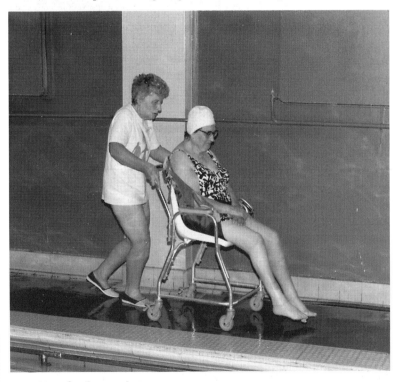

51   *Use of a shower chair*

Moving and assisting

Whenever you can, encourage the swimmer to use his own ability as far as possible, whether travelling to and from the pool, changing or at the poolside. This fosters the spirit of independence which is an integral part of the AST philosophy.

If you need advice on moving or assisting a specific swimmer and you do not have the expertise within the club, contact the swimmer's own therapist, if he has one. Alternatively, contact the local physiotherapy department and ask if a physiotherapist would be willing to come and give advice.

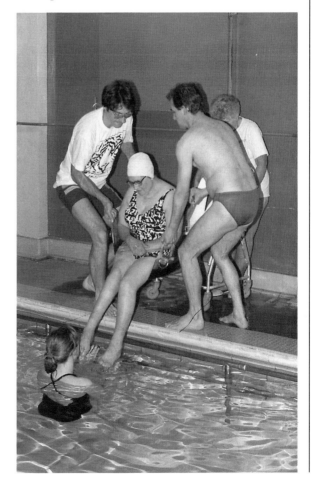

52 Use of a canvas lifting seat

Lifting

Avoid lifting if this is at all possible. First see whether you can use shower chairs, graduated stools, transfer boards or other equipment before lifting a swimmer. When you do need to lift, the use of a canvas lifting seat can make a lift safer and more comfortable for everybody.

Remember that lifting is a skill and should be taught and practised with supervision. Poor technique can put both swimmer and helpers at risk. Two or more people lifting correctly helps to minimise the strain.

Tips

- Do not lift unnecessarily.
- Discuss with the swimmer his needs, and encourage self-help where possible.
- Plan and prepare before you assist.
- Do not assist or lift if you feel you cannot manage it.
- Work within your own limitations and do not hesitate to ask for help if necessary.
- Think about your own body position while giving assistance – lifting is a significant factor in causing back pain.

15

Safety

All swimming pool sessions are potentially dangerous. It is essential that pool rules are strictly enforced for both swimmers and instructors. Some general safety guidelines will apply for all of your swimming sessions: more specific rules will depend on the particular circumstances. It is the responsibility of each club to make sure that its members know the safety regulations, and that they are practised regularly.

Personnel

To ensure that a swimming session is as safe as it is possible to make it, there must be a sufficient number of helpers to cope with any foreseeable emergency. At least one person present must be a qualified life saver. He should be on the poolside, not involved in any other activity. If this life-saver is responsible for more than just your own group of swimmers, or if you have a large group, then other spotters should be on the poolside as well. You may also need additional spotters if you have in your group swimmers who are oblivious to the risks involved in swimming. For example, some people may be unaware of the hazards of wandering into deep water.

Extra poolside observers may also be necessary if some of the swimmers have conditions which may cause sudden crises, such as diabetes, epilepsy or coronary difficulties. There should be someone on hand who knows about each relevant condition and the swimmers concerned. Records for each swimmer should be kept on the poolside to keep track of any problems which he might have. These should contain the phone number of the swimmer's doctor, for use both in a medical emergency and to answer questions which the chief instructor may have about any special precautions which need to be taken. A contact number for the swimmer's next of kin should also be in the records.

In addition, there should be someone present who is qualified in first aid. This may be the life-saver, or one of the spotters, or one of the instructors. In fact, all instructors are encouraged to train in first aid and resuscitation, as well as life-saving.

All swimmers and instructors must be familiar with the following emergency drill.

- The life-saver or person in charge blows a whistle (and waves a flag if there are hearing impaired swimmers or instructors in the group).
- Everyone in the water stays still and listens for instructions.
- Everyone moves quickly to the side when told to do so.

The drill should be practised frequently. This is especially important in a programme that includes swimmers with learning difficulties, who may not attend easily to the whistle.

Facilities

Although relatively few pools have been built specifically for use by people with disabilities, the average swimming pool can usually be easily adapted. You must check that the correct safety precautions have been taken: you must have access to a phone, and a first-aid kit should be close at hand. It would also be useful to have 'space blankets' or extra towels available if needed. In addition, check the following.

Doors

Doors in and around the pool area should always be unlocked during swimming sessions to allow for a fast and safe exit if there is an emergency. They should be left either completely open or completely shut: never leave a door ajar because some of your swimmers may have a visual disability. Be sure that exits are unblocked and that swimmers and instructors know the building's emergency procedures. Visually disabled participants should be made aware of the fire exits (as well as other aspects of the facilities) when they begin taking part in the sessions. Doors should be locked at the end of the session to avoid accidents from unsupervised use of the pool, unless another group is using it.

Changing rooms

Changing rooms should be uncluttered and have plenty of space to take wheelchairs, swimmers and helpers. The floor should be non-slip, and hot water pipes should be covered. An instructor or helper should be in the changing rooms whenever they are being used.

Poolside

A wet poolside is hazardous for everyone, but particularly for people with balance or other mobility problems. Keep the pool surroundings as free of clutter as possible. If you are going to use toys or other equipment in your session, store these well away from the poolside. Instructors in the water can ask for them when they need them. This applies also to wheelchairs and mobility aids. As in any swimming session, there should be no running, pushing or playing around which might be a danger to oneself or others.

Water depth

For swimmers needing support, the water should ideally be around 1.2 m (4 ft) deep. If it is any deeper, instructors will not have the stability to support the swimmers who need it, and standing in shallower water can be difficult when balance is poor. Also, many people with a disability swim with their bodies angled at 45° to the water surface, and so may find that they scrape their toes or feet if the water is not deep enough. Shallower water may be used for children.

Diving should never be taught in water with a vertical depth of less than 1.8 m (6 ft); at this depth the dive taught should be a flat racing dive only. For further recommendations on diving read *Diving in Swimming Pools* by the Institute of Baths and Recreation Management (IBRM). When diving or jumping in, be sure to check that no one is in the way. Swimmers with learning difficulties may need close supervision to help them make sure that the water is clear. Keep reminding them to 'Look' and 'Check'.

Other factors

There are other factors, too, which can help make the sessions a safer and more pleasant experience for everyone involved.

The method used by the AST states that swimmers should become adjusted to the water without any aids whatsoever. This encourages their confidence in their own abilities. Neither swimmers nor instructors, therefore, should wear goggles or nose clips. The exception would be where it is medically necessary, say, for some swimmers to wear goggles. Some glaucoma sufferers, for instance, wear permanent contact lenses and need to protect these from the water. These swimmers should bring a doctor's note explaining that goggles are necessary. However, nose clips should never be worn because they interfere with the learning of breath control.

Instructors, helpers and swimmers should remove all of their jewellery before working in or out of the water because they could easily scratch or cut, even quite severely. Many people with disabilities have circulation problems which mean that even a slight graze can take a long time to heal, and may become infected easily. The ban should include necklaces, bracelets, watches, rings (except wedding rings if they are smooth) and ear-rings (including stud earrings). Finger-nails can be an even greater threat to a swimmer's skin than jewellery – short, jagged nails can be as dangerous as long nails.

While it is inadvisable to swim while hungry, no one should eat immediately before swimming. Diabetic swimmers, however, will need to keep up their blood sugar levels, and so some source of sugar should be available on the poolside in case hyporglycaemia should occur. Ask swimmers or companions to have available the most appropriate form of sugar.

Neither swimmers nor instructors should chew gum. It can be easily inhaled, resulting in choking.

Rules and insurance

All instructors and helpers should be familiar with the rules which govern their sessions, whether they be the rules of the pool in which the session takes place, or the rules of the Education or Health Authority. Also, it is essential that both swimmers and instructors have suitable insurance cover in the event of an accident on the swimming pool premises. (There is an AST leaflet which provides details of the coverage available to AST-affiliated groups.) Be aware of your legal responsibilities.

16

Instructor training

If the heart of the AST is its clubs, then the swimmers and all the helpers are its life blood, and the latter need proper training to be able to contribute fully. This training must be sufficiently flexible to fulfil each individual's role in the club, and it must be appropriate for their personal level of interest and commitment. A helper in the changing rooms will require different training from club officials or administrators, who in turn need a programme distinct from that of a water instructor. For them all, first knowledge then experience will help to ensure the safety of both swimmers and instructors. Since the club is the place where training is needed, this is the sensible place for it to start, at the very first session. In the early stages, tuition should be informal, consisting of:

- introductory notes
- oral tuition from an experienced instructor
- a period of time spent learning by example and gaining hands-on experience under the supervision of experienced instructors.

Who does the training?

Within each club there should be some senior instructors who are divided into 'group leaders', 'tutor instructors' and 'chief instructors'.

The tutor instructor is responsible for organising training at the pool and making sure that training facilities are available for any new helpers. The tutor instructor is most likely to be one of the most experienced instructors in the club. Larger clubs may be able to provide all the basic training needs themselves.

In areas where there are several clubs in one town, or where clubs do not have the expertise to cover basic training needs, groups may come together to share resources. Single clubs or clubs formed in areas where there is little local support or no immediate neighbouring club will have to call on national officials to meet their basic training needs.

119

Whatever the circumstances training is essential, otherwise neither the swimmers nor the instructors will make any progress. It may be tempting to muddle through and pick up things as you go along, or to restrict club intake to experienced swimmers, but this is not good enough. One of the main strengths of the AST is its educational structure. It guarantees that common standards of teaching and assessment are found throughout the country, so that a swimmer may move happily from one club to another knowing that the content and pattern of teaching will be reassuringly familiar.

Using the Halliwick Method

Although it is not essential to understand all the complexities of the Halliwick Method to be a competent instructor, trainees do need to know the basic principles and philosophy: the use of games and groups, one-to-one swimmer-instructor ratio, the importance of communication and mental adjustment, the absence of artificial flotation aids, and so on.

Apart from the experience gained initially by working with other instructors immediately after joining, the level of training an instructor undertakes is at his own discretion. The AST recommends that all instructors should try to attain some practical experience in first aid, life-saving skills, basic resuscitation, and moving and assisting. Although there is no compulsion to do so, all new instructors are encouraged to attend at least a basic course on the Halliwick Method. They should be doing this not because they have to, but because they want to.

What is on offer?

The AST offers structured education and assessment for its instructors, both regionally and nationally, in a number of ways.

Learning in the club

The initial training which takes place in the potential instructor's own club is where he will learn:

- about the club structure
- about its place within the larger organisation of the AST

- teaching techniques for use in groups and with individuals
- how to communicate with swimmers with a disability
- how to assist them in the water and on the poolside.

This may or may not be on a structured basis, depending on the size of the club, the length of time it has been running, and its commitment to education. Unless the club has an established training programme regularly catering for the needs of new instructors, it is likely that the new member will have to learn on his own or with a couple of others.

The basic course

There are obvious advantages in a group of people coming together to learn about the Halliwick Method in a more formal setting. Such a setting is ideal to teach the Halliwick Method basic course. It is split into two parts – A and B – each of which covers both theory and practical group work, in and out of the water.

Depending on such considerations as the available venue, the catchment area of the candidates, and their own free time, the course can be run over two weekends, over four or five consecutive days, or over a series of evenings. Certain minimum criteria are laid down for the lecture and water times. The courses themselves are conducted only by accredited AST lecturers.

The syllabus

Part A

Theory
Introduction.
History and philosophy of the Halliwick Method.
Why no flotation aids?
Effects of water.
Disability outline/handicap effect.
Ten point programme.
Breath control.
Four aspects of rotation.
Moving and assisting on land.
Poolside safety.
Care of swimmer.

AST structure.
Video: 'Water Free'.
Group discussion and question time.

Pool work
Basic supports.
Balance and rotations.
The moving body.
Demonstrations of effects of water.
Demonstrations of group work for different abilities and ages.

Part B

Theory
Introduction.
Ten point programme.
Groups and grouping.
Games/activities and their objectives.
Teaching techniques.
Review of games.
Programmes for progress.
Singing, music and movement.
Competition.
AST proficiency awards.
Group exercises and discussion.

Pool work
Revision of basic supports.
AST proficiency awards.
Groups for different abilities and ages.
Group demonstrations: games based on ten point programme, and games based on proficiency awards

Parts A and B should not be less than 12 hours each, with a minimum of four hours water work and eight hours lecture and discussion time. The AST issues numbered certificates of attendance at all its courses, and those for both A and B courses are a prerequisite for all further courses or application for assessment.

Most instructors do not feel the need to go beyond the basic course, which is designed to give them enough working knowledge to instruct under the guidance of a group leader.

Progression

For those who want to train beyond the basics, there is a complete range of courses available, again staffed by AST accredited lecturers. Some courses are largely informative with a practical element to support the lectures, while others are directed at equipping the instructor for a particular role or position within the AST club structure. This latter group includes tuition for group leaders, tutor instructors, demonstrators and lecturers.

Gaining the instructor's certificate

The Halliwick Instructor's Certificate is a certificate of competence issued to instructors who have:

- worked at least 100 hours with swimmers in the water
- attended a basic course A and B
- successfully undergone an assessment covering their practical work in the water with a range of swimmers with disabilities
- successfully undergone an assessment of their understanding of the Halliwick Method.

This certificate qualifies instructors to teach in group situations under the direction of a group leader.

A system already exists for supporting and assessing potential lecturers, and the AST hopes to extend this to new demonstrators.

Specific skills

For those who have completed the basic course and do not want a new role in their clubs, but do want to improve their knowledge and practical ability, there is a progressive range of courses covering various aspects of the Halliwick Method in greater detail. These are:

- 'Games and their objectives'
- 'Groups and grouping'
- 'Programmes for progress'.

The AST also offers a number of specialist courses:

- 'Moving and assisting on land'
- 'Stroke technique'
- 'Gala organisation'.

In fact, the first of the specialist courses, although aimed more at movement in the changing area and to and from the poolside, is recommended to *all* instructors and is run by AST lecturers with specific skills in this area.

Seminar and discussion

The AST's education teams are constantly responding to demands for information as clubs and individuals pose new questions or as new techniques are developed. To answer these needs the association holds annual seminars which are open to all members. Here, the association reviews various topics, often with the help of visiting speakers.

There are also regular discussion groups which meet to consider the various new developments which have been brought to the AST's attention.

More information

Details of the current courses are available from either the Education Secretary or the National Secretary, whose addresses are given on page 126. Members of national education teams are always pleased to help wherever they can by providing introductory talks and showing the association's video tapes to interested groups, or by running full courses.

Further reading

Teaching swimming to people with special needs

Booklets produced by the National Co-ordinating Committee on Swimming for People with Disabilities (NCCSPD):

1 'Forming a Club'
2 'Lifting and Handling'
3 'Swimming and Epilepsy'
4 'Facilities'
5 'Medical Considerations'
6 'Classification Systems in Competitive Swimming'.

Available from John Hughes (Secretary, NCCSPD), 3 Knoll Crescent, Northwood, Middlesex HA6 1HH

Anyone Can Swim – Amateur Swimming Association (ASA), edited by Joan Harrison (Crowood Press)

Hydrotherapy in Paediatrics – M. Reid Campion (William Heinemann Medical Books)

In the Pool – Swimming Instruction for the Disabled (Oslo Publications). Available from the Swimming Teachers' Association (STA), Anchor House, Birch Street, Walsall WS2 8HZ

Manual for Teaching Swimming to the Disabled (Canadian Red Cross). Available from the STA (address above)

Swimming for Life – The Therapy of Swimming – Ronald Russell (Pelham Books)

'Teaching the Disabled to Swim' (training notes for helpers by the National Association of Swimming Clubs for the Handicapped (NASCH). Available from Rosemary O'Leary (Administrative Officer), NASCH Administrative Office, The Willows, Mayles Lane, Wickham, Hampshire PO17 5ND

The Teaching of Swimming for Those With Special Needs (ASA). Available from Mrs M. Avery, Harold Fern House, Derby Square, Loughborough, Leicestershire LE11 0AL

'Working with Young Children Using the Halliwick Method' (pamphlet produced by the Association of Swimming Therapy). Available from Mr J.A. Jandrell (Treasurer), 261 Christchurch Road, Newport, Gwent NP9 8BE

Games and activities

Swimming Games and Activities – Alan Creegan and Jim Noble (A & C Black)

Moving and assisting

The Handling of Patients (The Back Pain Association in collaboration with the Royal College of Nursing)

Safety and Lifesaving

Aquatic Lifesaving for Supervisors of People with Disabilities – edited by Olive Bowes (The Royal Life Saving Society). Available from Mountbatten House, Studley, Warwickshire B80 7NN

Diving in Swimming Pools (The Institute of Baths and Recreation Management). Available from Giffard House, 36/38 Sherrard Street, Melton Mowbray, Leicestershire LE13 1XJ

Safety in Swimming Pools (Health and Safety Commission). Available from The Sports Council, 16 Upper Woburn Place, London WC1H 0QP

Videos

The following videos are available from Concord Film and Video Library, 201 Felixstowe Road, Ipswich, Suffolk IP3 9BJ.

'Breathtaking' (for hire or purchase)

'The Halliwick Method' (for hire only)

'Water Free' (for hire or purchase)

Useful addresses

Association of Swimming Therapy
Ted Cowen (Hon. Sec.), 4 Oak Street, Shrewsbury SY3 7RH

Mrs P. J. Scott (Education Sec.), 42 Goodhew Close, Yapton, West Sussex BN18 0JA

Olive Lee (Hon. Equipment Sec.), 4 St Mary's Place, Portskewett, Newport, Gwent NP6 4UD

Amateur Swimming Association
Convener of the Working Party for Swimming for People with Disabilities, Harold Fern House, Derby Square, Loughborough, Leicestershire LE11 0AL

British Sports Association for the Disabled
34 Osnaburgh Street, London NW1 3ND

Canvas lifting seat
Available from JMC Rehab Ltd, 1 Hogg Street, Airdrie, Scotland

National Association of Swimming Clubs for the Handicapped
Rosemary O'Leary (Administrative Officer), NASCH Administrative
Office, The Willows, Mayles Lane, Wickham, Hampshire PO17 5ND

**National Co-ordinating Committee on Swimming
for People with Disabilities**
John Hughes (Secretary), 3 Knoll Crescent, Northwood, Middlesex
HA6 1HH

Royal Life Saving Society
Olive Bowes, Mountbatten House, Studley, Warwickshire B80 7NN

Swimming Teachers' Association
Nigel Brailsford, Anchor House, Birch Street, Walsall WS2 8HZ

Index